SPECIAL TECHNIQUES IN
EXCEL

SPECIAL TECHNIQUES IN
EXCEL

David Fong

PARTRIDGE

Print information available on the last page.

To order additional copies of this book, contact
Toll Free 800 101 2657 (Singapore)
Toll Free 1 800 81 7340 (Malaysia)
orders.singapore@partridgepublishing.com

www.partridgepublishing.com/singapore

CONTENTS

Introduction...vii

Chapter 1   Understanding Functions.. 1
Chapter 2   Query with Grouping Data......................................29
Chapter 3   Query with Approximate Matching.........................47
Chapter 4   Query with Random Data 65
Chapter 5   Query with Two Conditions 83
Chapter 6   Dynamic Text..107
Chapter 7   Dynamic Total 121
Chapter 8   Dynamic Nonduplicate List...................................133

INTRODUCTION

Overview

Excel is the most common computational tool in the world. However, at the present time I have seen many Excel users use Excel only as a simple computational tool. Mostly, the data are manually keyed in to create periodical reports. This is because many think Excel cannot perform query operations like other computation tools. In most Excel users' knowledge, Excel can only perform simple queries by using either VLOOKUP, HLOOKUP, INDEX, or OFFSET functions. In these simple queries, only one piece of data is retrieved upon one or multiple conditions. It seems that there is no such query for extracting all the related data upon one condition (or multiple conditions) in Excel.

This book offers new query techniques that can extract all related data with a given condition or multiple conditions in the specified range. Thus, Excel will have a new query tool for performing automated data. In this book, I will show Excel users that they can perform query operations with the given condition. The techniques are called special techniques, and I developed them through more than ten years of experience using Excel.

These query techniques open a new platform for Excel users to perform automated data analysis or solution generation, and it is equally powerful compared to others computation tools. These techniques will become common tools to the common computation tool in the world that is Excel.

Benefits

The special techniques in Excel will provide a new platform for Excel users to operate. These techniques will provide numerous benefits.

a) Data analysis will be fully automated from key-in until reporting, with a single condition or multiple conditions.

b) By having automated data, we will save memory in saving the whole data, let's say up to one year of data. All the database data will be saved in one worksheet.

c) With the same data, we can create daily, weekly, monthly, or yearly reports at will. This report will be only on one sheet, which I called an active sheet. It changes upon the condition changed.

d) The report is an active sheet, and thus it is tidy and need. We do not need to find the report from many files or worksheets; simply use the query condition.

e) Because the workload in preparing this report will be a data-entry job, then, we can have the opportunity to save manpower in preparing the reports.

f) Once it is set up, the report technique will be accurate for daily, weekly, monthly, or yearly reports.

g) The old report can be obtained within minutes by keying in the condition. This will save time in response to the customer requests.

How to Use This Book

The book provides new query techniques in Excel. I try my best to put it in as simple a manner as possible so that a new user in Excel can understand and perform the query operation by following it closely.

Chapter 1 is an introduction to more advance functions in Excel. By understanding these functions, the users can have a rough idea of query techniques.

Chapter 2 opens a new query understanding in Excel. I call it Query with Grouping Data. This technique is useful for daily reports or creating automated invoices or delivery orders.

Chapter 3 is similar to chapter 2, but the difference is that the query condition is an approximate matching rather than exact matching. It is useful for monthly data or daily machine data.

Chapter 4 is about querying random data. However, it can also perform as a query with grouping data. I sometimes prefer the query with grouping data because it saves memory in extracting the grouping data. This technique is useful for stock information, man information, or sales information. It can perform similar operation as in chapters 2 and 3, but it will use up higher memory.

Chapter 5 is the extension of the query techniques whereby two conditions are used. It can also be used for more than two conditions.

In the earlier chapters, I demonstrate how to perform query operation. In automated data solution, once we have performed query for automated data, we will present it in a most presentable way. We cannot always change the format manually. Thus, chapter 6 offers a way to perform dynamic text. This will work best with all the query techniques.

Chapter 7 is a new technique that opens the automated formatting for display purposes. Sometimes upon query, we need to put a total or a summary just below the extracted data. This is the technique to do it.

Chapter 8 is about making summaries related to nonduplicate lists. Sometimes upon query, we need to have a list of items to be presented in a monthly summary report. Thus, the automated nonduplicate list technique will be able to help.

I hope these special techniques in Excel become a versatile platform for users. I have used it, and it greatly improves Excel.

History

In this section, I will share my experience as to how I developed these techniques through the years. I believe that simply by understanding the development, users will be able to have confidence to master the special techniques in Excel for better automated data solutions.

About ten years ago, I developed Query with Grouping Data. I used this to automate invoices and delivery orders, which helped my customers save time and manpower in preparing these reports.

Three months later, I developed the Query with Approximate Matching technique for my customers in preparing automated monthly and weekly reports for productivity presentations. I also make use of this technique to perform daily data analysis for the real-time machine data. It saves time and is very presentable.

With these two techniques, I can help my customers. However, when it comes to random data found, such as in defective items presentation, I was blanked. In 2011, I managed to develop the first technique for Query with Random Data. I managed to use the ROW and RANK function to create this technique. It was a breakthrough to me in developing this technique. Then six months later, I developed a similar technique, making use of the COUNTIF function.

With these three techniques, I can perform any kind of data analysis given to me by my customers. The techniques seem complete as far as query is concerned. However, usually upon query, customers requested to put a total or summary below the extracted data. This technique is called dynamic formatting, and it took another three months to develop.

The last technique, Query with Nonduplicate List, is also a kind of formatting method. It took me one year to think of this. I should have developed it earlier through the random technique that makes use of the COUNTIF function.

I hope that you do not take long to master these special techniques. You will be fully equipped with these special techniques, and soon you may be able to formulate better ones.

CHAPTER 1

Understanding Functions

1.0 Overview

There are many functions in Excel. Maybe some of you all already familiar with the functions. Here, I just covered the necessary Excel functions to develop the special techniques.

Please note that my explanation for the given functions might not be a complete one. However, the explanation just suits the requirements to develop the special technique. If you wanted to explore further for details explanation to the function, you can always seek the Excel Help in the Excel spreadsheet itself.

I will cover the below functions. Simple functions such as SUM or WEEKNUM will not be covered in this book.

IF
COUNTIF
MATCH
INDEX
RANK
VLOOKUP
HLOOKUP
IFERROR
TEXT

The explanation of the functions shall include the following.

a) Function Syntax
b) Function Operation
c) Example

1.1 IF

a) Function Syntax
=IF (condition, return value if condition true, return value if condition false)

    i) Condition refers to the equation comparing two cells, usually a data cell with the assigned cell.

    ii) Return value if the condition is true means that Excel will return a value or execute the function written.

    iii) Return value if the condition is false means that Excel will return a value or execute the function written.

b) Function Operation
The IF function will compare two cells and will return the value according to whether it is true or false.

c) Example 1

    i) Key in "Bill" in cell A1.

    ii) Create a formula in cell C1 as below. This is the simplest IF function I've ever come across.
        =IF(A1="","",A1)

    iii) The breakdown of the IF block is as below.
        condition => A1=""
        if condition true => ""
        if condition false => A1

    iv) The function is comparing whether cell A1 is blank ("") or not. If it is blank then it return the blank; and if it is not blank then it return the value in cell A1. This is called blanking. In a later chapter, you will notice a lot of blanking.

v)   In this case, it returns "Bill" in cell C1 as below.

	A	B	C
1	Bill		Bill

vi)   For simulation, delete cell A1. You will get a blank in cell C1.

d)   Example 2

i)   Key in "123" in cell A1.
ii)   Create a formula in cell C1 as below.
=IF(A1<=0,"complete","open")
iii)   Press Enter. You obtain the following in range A1:C1.

	A	B	C
1	123		open

iv)   Key in "c" in cell B1.
v)   Change the formula in cell C1 as below.
=IF(B1="c","closed",IF(A1<=0,"complete","open"))
vi)   The above formula is a nested IF function. The first IF function, as in step ii, becomes the result of the second IF function when the condition is false. Take note of the syntax of the IF function.
vii)   Press Enter. You obtain the following in range A1:C1.

	A	B	C
1	123	c	closed

viii)   Delete value in cell A1 and B1. You obtain the following in range A1:C1.

3

	A	B	C
1			complete

ix) Key in "1" in cell A1. You obtain the following in range A1:C1.

	A	B	C
1	1		open

1.2 COUNTIF

a) Function Syntax
=COUNTIF (range, condition)

   i) Range refers to the data to be counted.
   ii) Condition refers to the criteria required in the assigned cell.

b) Function Operation

The function returns a number of data where the range matches the condition.

c) Example 1

   i) Let's say we have data in range A1:A8 as below.

	A
1	April
2	April
3	Bill
4	April
5	Bill
6	Cherrie
7	Cherrie
8	April

4

ii) Then we put a condition in cell D1. Key in "April".

iii) To count the number of data related to "April", we create a formula in cell B1 as below.

=COUNTIF(A1:A8,D1)

iv) You obtain a value of 4; thus, 4 data.

v) You obtain the following in range A1:D8.

	A	B	C	D
1	April	4		April
2	April			
3	Bill			
4	April			
5	Bill			
6	Cherrie			
7	Cherrie			
8	April			

d) Example 2

i) In the above example, we only count with a single cell. Sometimes we need to count for the whole range. To do this, we use the same data in example 1.

ii) With the condition in cell D1, create a formula in cell B1 as below.

=COUNTIF(A1:A1,D1)

Press Enter we obtain a value of 1. Thus, there is only 1 data. This is because we used the range as A1:A1.

iii) Put absolute value to the range A1:A1 as below.

=COUNTIF($A$1:A1,$D$1)

iv) Notice that we just put a dollar sign for the first cell A1. This means we locked the first cell A1. By locking, when we copy downwards, the first cell A1 will not change, but the second cell A1 will change accordingly (to A2, A3, and so on.) Notice also that we locked cell D1 because we wanted to compare with the condition in this cell.

v) Copy cell B1 to range B2:B8. You obtain the following in range A1:D8.

	A	B	C	D
1	April	1		April
2	April	2		
3	Bill	2		
4	April	3		
5	Bill	3		
6	Cherrie	3		
7	Cherrie	3		
8	April	4		

vi) Sometimes we simply want to see only the data that are related to "April". Thus, we need to use the IF function to do the comparison. Change the formula in cell B1 as below. Take note of the absolute value of cell D1.

=IF(A1=$D$1,COUNTIF($A$1:A1,$D$1),"")

vii) Take note that in the IF function block, we can break down the function as follows.

condition => A1=$D$1

if condition true => COUNTIF($A$1:A1,$D$1)

if condition false => ""

viii) In step vi, we actually performed blanking. This means putting blanks for unrelated data.

ix) You obtain the following in range A1:D8.

⊿	A	B	C	D
1	April	1		April
2	April	2		
3	Bill			
4	April	3		
5	Bill			
6	Cherrie			
7	Cherrie			
8	April	4		

1.3 MATCH

a) Function Syntax
    =MATCH (lookup value, range, type)

    i)   Lookup value refers to the cell you want to match with the given range.

    ii)   Range refers to the data or list for matching.

    iii) The type can be 0, 1, or -1. Here we will discuss 0 and 1 only.

    iv) 0 refers to an exact match.

    v)   1 refers to an approximate (less than) match. For this, the list must be in order.

    vi) 1 refers to approximate (less than) match. For this, the list must be in order.

b) Function Operation

    i)   The MATCH functions will return the row of the match data in the list.

    ii)   It acts as a pointer to find the data in the range.

    iii) For type 0, it will return the row of the first data in the list.

    iv) For type 1, it will return the row or the most approximate data in the list.

c) Example 1

i) Let's say we have data in range A1:A8 as below.
ii) We put condition in cell C1. Key in "coconut".

	A
1	apple
2	banana
3	coconut
4	kiwi
5	lemon
6	manggo
7	orange
8	papaya

iii) To find the row related to "coconut", we create a formula in cell C2 as below.
=MATCH(C1,A1:A8,0)

Press Enter we obtain a value of 3. This is the row of "coconut" in the list.

iv) You obtain the following in range A1:C8.

	A	B	C
1	apple		coconut
2	banana		3
3	coconut		
4	kiwi		
5	lemon		
6	manggo		
7	orange		
8	papaya		

v) For simulation, type "orange" in cell C1.
vi) You obtain the following in range A1:C8.

8

	A	B	C
1	apple		orange
2	banana		7
3	coconut		
4	kiwi		
5	lemon		
6	manggo		
7	orange		
8	papaya		

vii) Now change cell A5 from "lemon" to "orange".

viii) You obtain the following in range A1:C8.

	A	B	C
1	apple		orange
2	banana		5
3	coconut		
4	kiwi		
5	orange		
6	manggo		
7	orange		
8	papaya		

ix) Notice that the value in cell C2 changes to 5. This is because the MATCH will take the row of the first data that match.

d) Example 2

   i) Let's say we have data in range A1:A8 as below.

	A
1	1-Mar
2	4-Mar
3	7-Mar
4	10-Mar
5	13-Mar
6	16-Mar
7	19-Mar
8	22-Mar
9	25-Mar
10	28-Mar

ii) We put a condition in cell C2. Key in "1-Mar".

iii) To find the row related to "1-Mar", we create a formula in cell D2 as below. This is an exact match.

=MATCH(C2,A1:A10,0)

iv) Press Enter we obtain a value of 1. This is the row of "1-Mar" in the list.

v) Create a formula in cell E2 as below. This is an approximate match.

=MATCH(C2,A1:A10,1)

vi) Notice the difference between the formula in iii and v.

vii) You obtain the following in range A1:E8.

	A	B	C	D	E
1	1-Mar		Date	Exact	Approx
2	4-Mar		1-Mar	1	1
3	7-Mar				
4	10-Mar				
5	13-Mar				
6	16-Mar				
7	19-Mar				
8	22-Mar				
9	25-Mar				
10	28-Mar				

viii) Change the date in cell C2 to "9-Mar".

ix) You obtain the following in range A1:E8.

	A	B	C	D	E
1	1-Mar		Date	Exact	Approx
2	4-Mar		9-Mar	#N/A	3
3	7-Mar				
4	10-Mar				
5	13-Mar				
6	16-Mar				
7	19-Mar				
8	22-Mar				
9	25-Mar				
10	28-Mar				

x) Notice that for the exact match, the result is #NA, and for the approximate match, the result is 3. This is right because row 4 in the list is "10-Mar".

1.4 INDEX

a) Function Syntax
=INDEX (range, row number, column number)

i) Range refers to the data from which you wanted to extract.
ii) Row number refers to the row of the above range.
iii) Column number refers to the column of the above range.

b) Function Operation

i) The INDEX function extracts required data from the range with reference to the row and column given.
ii) It acts as an extractor to pull data. Thus, it works perfectly with the MATCH function, because MATCH acts as a pointer.

c) Example 1

i) Let's say we have data in range A1:B8 as below.

	A	B
1	ID No	Name
2	6186369	April
3	7422814	Bill
4	6743995	Cherrie
5	4783710	David
6	8099707	Euwe
7	3693507	Frances
8	6040476	Gillian

ii) Create a formula in cell D1 as below.
=INDEX(A1:B8,2,2)
iii) This INDEX function extracts the intersection of row 2 and column data from range A1:B8. Thus, the result is "April".
iv) Let us put 3 in cell D2 and 3 in cell E2.
v) Create a formula in cell D4 as below.
=INDEX(A1:B8,D2,E2)
vi) You obtain #REF!. This is because the range only has two columns.
vii) Change the value of cell E2 to 1.
viii) You obtain the following in range A1:E8.

	A	B	C	D	E
1	ID No	Name		row	column
2	6186369	April		3	1
3	7422814	Bill		result	
4	6743995	Cherrie		7422814	
5	4783710	David			
6	8099707	Euwe			
7	3693507	Frances			
8	6040476	Gillian			

d) Example 2

    i)   Let's say we have data in range A1:B8 as below.

	A	B
1	ID No	Name
2	6186369	April
3	7422814	Bill
4	6743995	Cherrie
5	4783710	David
6	8099707	Euwe
7	3693507	Frances
8	6040476	Gillian

    ii)   We want to find the ID No with the given name.

    iii)   Let's key in "David" in cell D1.

    iv)   Create a formula in cell D2 as below.
=MATCH(D1,B1:B8,0)

    v)   This is to find the row related to "David". You obtain value of 5. This is row 5.

    vi)   Create a formula in cell D3 as below.
=INDEX(A1:A8,D2,0)

    vii)   You obtain the following in range A1:D8.

	A	B	C	D
1	ID No	Name		David
2	6186369	April		5
3	7422814	Bill		4783710
4	6743995	Cherrie		
5	4783710	David		
6	8099707	Euwe		
7	3693507	Frances		
8	6040476	Gillian		

viii) The same result (4783710) can also be obtained by creating a composite formula in cell D5 as below.
=INDEX(A1:A8,MATCH(D1,B1:B8,0),0)

ix) In the above formula, the MATCH function supplies the row number for the INDEX function.

x) You obtain the following in range A1:D8.

	A	B	C	D
1	ID No	Name		David
2	6186369	April		5
3	7422814	Bill		4783710
4	6743995	Cherrie		
5	4783710	David		4783710
6	8099707	Euwe		
7	3693507	Frances		
8	6040476	Gillian		

xi) The formula in cell D5 is a sort of lookup, but in this case, it is a lookup to the left.

1.5 RANK

a) Function Syntax
=RANK(value, list, order)

i) Value refers to the number you want to rank.
ii) List refers to the column of the number you want to rank.
iii) Order =1 implies ascending, and 0 implies descending.

b) Function Operation

The RANK function will rank value in the list in ascending or descending order.

c) Example 1

i) Let's say we have data in range A1:B8 as below.

	A
1	55
2	5
3	88
4	66
5	29
6	85
7	74
8	53

ii) Create a formula in cell B1 as below.
=RANK(A1,A1:A8,0)
iii) Put the absolute value as below.
=RANK(A1,$A$1:$A$8,0)
iv) Copy cell B1 to range B2:B8.
v) Create a formula in cell C1 with absolute value as below.
=RANK(A1,$A$1:$A$8,1)
vi) You obtain the following in range A1:C8.

	A	B	C
1	55	5	4
2	5	8	1
3	88	1	8
4	66	4	5
5	29	7	2
6	85	2	7
7	74	3	6
8	53	6	3

    vii)   Notice that the rank between column B and column C.

1.6 VLOOKUP

a) Function Syntax
=VLOOKUP(lookup value, range, column number, sorting)

    i)   Lookup value refers to the cell you want to find in the range.
    ii)   Range refers to the database for lookup.
    iii)   Column refers to the column of the range counting from the leftmost.
    iv)   Sorting refers to whether or not your range is in order. It has a value of 0 or 1. A 0 implies the range no need to be sorted, and the lookup is an exact one. A 1 or an omitted input implies the range must be sorted, and the lookup is approximate.

b) Function Operation

    i)   The VLOOKUP function will look up in the leftmost column of the range by a given condition.
    ii)   It will return a single result in the formula cell.
    iii)   It has two types, exact or approximate.

c) Example 1

    i)   Let's say we have data in range A1:C7 as below.

	A	B	C
1	Mark		Grade
2	from	to	
3	0	39.9	F
4	40	54.9	D
5	55	69.9	C
6	70	84.9	B
7	85	100	A

ii) Key in 88 in cell E2.

iii) Create a formula in cell F2 as below.
=VLOOKUP(E2,A3:C7,3,1)

iv) Press Enter. You obtain a result of "A".

v) Notice that the value you look up is 88, which is not in the range, but is greater than 70 and less than 85. VLOOKUP still returns the result of "A".

vi) Notice that the sort = 1. Omit 1 in the below formula. You still obtain the same result, "A".
=VLOOKUP(E2,A3:C7,3)

vii) Put sort = 0, and you obtain #N/A. That is because with sort = 0, VLOOKUP looks for 88.

d) Example 2

i) Let say we have data in range A1:C8 as below.

	A	B	C
1	Name	Sex	Age
2	April	F	33
3	Bill	M	29
4	Cherrie	F	33
5	David	M	27
6	Euwe	M	29
7	Frances	F	28
8	Gillian	F	39

ii)   Key in "David" in cell F1.
iii) Create a formula in cell F2 as below.
      =VLOOKUP(F1,A2:C8,2,0)
iv)   Create a formula in cell F3 as below.
      =VLOOKUP(F1,A2:C8,3,0)
v)   Notice that the difference between the formula in cell F2 and cell F3 is the column number.
vi)   You obtain the following in range A1:F8.

	A	B	C	D	E	F
1	Name	Sex	Age		Name	David
2	April	F	33		Sex	M
3	Bill	M	29		Age	27
4	Cherrie	F	33			
5	David	M	27			
6	Euwe	M	29			
7	Frances	F	28			
8	Gillian	F	39			

e)   Example 3

i)   Let's say we have data in range A1:C8 as below.

	A	B	C	D	E	F
1	Name	Sex	Race		Shortform	Race
2	April	F	ENG		CHN	Chinese
3	Bill	M	CHN		ENG	English
4	Cherrie	F	CHN		IND	Indian
5	David	M	ENG			
6	Euwe	M	IND		Shortform	Sex
7	Frances	F	IND		F	Female
8	Gillian	F	ENG		M	Male

ii)   We wanted to know the race and sex of a given name in full.
iii) Key in "Bill" in cell I1.

iv) First create a formula in cell I2 as below.
=VLOOKUP(I1,A2:C8,2,0)

v) Press Enter. You obtain "M". This value will become a lookup value for the next VLOOKUP function.

vi) Change the formula in cell I2 to as below.
=VLOOKUP(VLOOKUP(I1,A2:C8,2,0),E7:F8,2)

vii) Press Enter. You obtain "Male" in cell I2.

viii) Similarly for cell I3, create a formula as below.
=VLOOKUP(VLOOKUP(I1,A2:C8,3,0),E2:F4,2,0)

ix) In this example, we notice that the VLOOKUP value can become a value for the next VLOOKUP function.

f) Example 4

i) Let's say we have data in range A1:C8 as below.

	A	B	C	D	E	F
1	Name	Sex	Race		Heading	Column
2	April	F	ENG		Sex	2
3	Bill	M	CHN		Race	3
4	Cherrie	F	CHN			
5	David	M	ENG			
6	Euwe	M	IND			
7	Frances	F	IND			
8	Gillian	F	ENG			

ii) We want to find either the sex or the race with the given name.

iii) Key in "David" and "Sex" in cells H1 and I1 respectively.

iv) First create a formula in cell I2 as below.
=MATCH(I1,A1:C1,0)

v) Press Enter. You obtain 2. This value will become the column number for the next VLOOKUP function.

vi) Change the formula in cell I2 to as below.
=VLOOKUP(H1,A2:C8,MATCH(I1,A1:C1,0),0)

vii) Press Enter. You obtain "M" in cell I2.

viii) Change the value in I1 to "Race".

ix) You obtain "ENG" in cell I2.
x) In this example we notice that MATCH value can become column number for the VLOOKUP function.
xi) You obtain the following in range H1:I2.

	H	I
1	David	Race
2		ENG

1.7 HLOOKUP

a) Function Syntax
=HLOOKUP(lookup value, range, row number, sorting)

i) Lookup value refers to the cell you want to find in the range.
ii) Range refers to the database for lookup.
iii) Column refers to the row of the range counting from the heading.
iv) Sorting refers to whether or not your range is in order. It has a value of 0 or 1. Usually we use 0.

b) Function Operation

i) The HLOOKUP function will look up at the heading and find the data downward of the range by a given condition.
ii) It will return a single result in the formula cell.

c) Example 1

i) Let's say we have data in range A1:G8 as below.

	A	B	C	D	E	F	G
1	Name	Sex	Age		Name	Sex	Age
2	April	F	33				
3	Bill	M	29				
4	Cherrie	F	33				
5	David	M	27				
6	Euwe	M	29				
7	Frances	F	28				
8	Gillian	F	39				

ii)   We want to extract data for the headings in range E1:G1.

iii) Key in 2 in cell D2.

iv)   Create a formula in cell E2 as below.
      =HLOOKUP(E1,A1:C8,2,0)

v)   You obtain "April" in cell E2.

vi)   Step (iv) is the simplest form of HLOOKUP function.

vii) Change the formula in cell E2 as below.
      =HLOOKUP(E1,A1:C8,D2,0)

viii) Notice that we put in a variable cell D2 for the column number.

ix)   Convert the formula to absolute, as below.
      =HLOOKUP(E$1,$A$1:$C$8,$D2,0)

x)   Copy cell E2 to range F2:G2.

xi)   You obtain the following in range D1:G2.

	D	E	F	G
1		Name	Sex	Age
2	2	April	F	33

xii) Notice that we extract data from row 2 of range A1:C8.

xiii) Change the value of cell D2 to 5.

xiv) You obtain the following in range D1:G2.

	D	E	F	G
1		Name	Sex	Age
2	5	David	M	27

xv) Key in 2, 4 and 6 in cells D2, D3 and D4 respectively.
xvi) Copy range E2:G2 to range E3:G4.
xvii) You obtain the following in range D1:G4.

	D	E	F	G
1		Name	Sex	Age
2	2	April	F	33
3	4	Cherrie	F	33
4	6	Euwe	M	29

d) Example 2

i) Let's say we have data in range A1:E7 as below.

	A	B	C	D	E
1	DO No.	Item	Description	QTY	UOM
2	A0001	1	pen	36	pcs
3	A0002	1	eraser	12	pcs
4	A0002	2	ruler	6	pcs
5	A0003	1	pencil	12	pcs
6	A0003	2	paper	6	rim
7	A0003	3	pen	24	pcs

ii) Key in "A0001" in cell G1.
iii) Create a formula in cell H1 as below.
=COUNTIF(A1:A7,G1)
iv) Press Enter. You obtain a value of 1. This is the count of "A0001" in range A1:A7.
v) Create a formula in cell H2 as below.
=MATCH(G1,A1:A7,0)

vi) Press Enter. You obtain a value of 2. This is the row of the first data.

vii) Create a formula in H3 as below.

=IF(G3<=H1,H2+1,"")

viii) Convert to absolute as below.

=IF(G3<=$H$1,H2+1,"")

ix) Copy cell H3 to cell H4.

x) You obtain the following in range G1:H4.

	G	H
1	A0001	1
2	1	2
3	2	
4	3	

xi) For simulation, change value of cell G1 to "A0002".

xii) You obtain the following in range G1:H4.

	G	H
1	A0002	2
2	1	3
3	2	4
4	3	

xiii) Copy heading range A1:E1 to range I1:M1.

xiv) Create a formula in cell I2 as below.

=HLOOKUP(I1,A1:E7,H2,0)

xv) Convert the formula to absolute value as below.

=HLOOKUP(I$1,$A$1:$E$7,$H2,0)

xvi) Copy cell I2 to range I2:M4.

xvii) You obtain the following in range I1:M4.

	I	J	K	L	M
1	DO No.	Item	Description	QTY	UOM
2	A0002	1	eraser	12	pcs
3	A0002	2	ruler	6	pcs
4	#REF!	#REF!	#REF!	#REF!	#REF!

xviii) You have already extract all the related data based on the condition "A0002".

xix) The #REF! is due to the fact there is no value in cell H4.

xx) Thus, we need to do blanking for these.

xxi) Change the formula in cell I2 as below.

=IF($H2="","",HLOOKUP(I$1,$A$1:$E$7,$H2,0))

xxii) Copy cell I2 to range I2:M4.

xxiii) You obtain the following in range I1:M4.

	I	J	K	L	M
1	DO No.	Item	Description	QTY	UOM
2	A0002	1	eraser	12	pcs
3	A0002	2	ruler	6	pcs
4					

xxiv) For simulation, change value in cell G1 to "A0003".

xxv) You obtain the following in range I1:M4.

	I	J	K	L	M
1	DO No.	Item	Description	QTY	UOM
2	A0003	1	pencil	12	pcs
3	A0003	2	paper	6	rim
4	A0003	3	pen	24	pcs

1.8 IFERROR

a) Function Syntax

=IFERROR(value, value if error)

i)   Value refers to the value to be tested.

ii)   Value if error is the return when error.

b)   Function Operation

     i)   The IFERROR function tests the value for error. If the value is not an error, it will return the same value. If the value is an error, it will return the value if it's an error.

c)   Example 1

     i)   The function =IFERROR(#N/A,0) will return a value of 0. This is because the term #N/A is an error.

     ii)   The function =IFERROR(1,0) will return a value of 1. This is because 1 is not an error.

d)   Example 2

     i)   Let's say we have data in range A1:E7 as below.

	A	B
1	Name	Sex
2	April	F
3	Bill	M
4	Cherrie	F
5	David	M
6	Euwe	M
7	Frances	F
8	Gillian	F

     ii)   Key in "Francis" in cell D1.

     iii)   Create a formula in cell E1 as below.
               =VLOOKUP(D1,A1:B8,2,0)

     iv)   You obtain the following in range A1:E8.

	A	B	C	D	E
1	Name	Sex		Francis	#N/A
2	April	F			
3	Bill	M			
4	Cherrie	F			
5	David	M			
6	Euwe	M			
7	Frances	F			
8	Gillian	F			

v) You obtain #N/A. This is because the name "Francis" is wrongly spelled. It should be "Frances".

vi) Key in "Bill" in cell D3.

vii) Create a formula in cell E1 as below.
=VLOOKUP(D3,A1:B8,3,0)

viii) You obtain the following in range A1:E8.

	A	B	C	D	E
1	Name	Sex		Francis	#N/A
2	April	F			
3	Bill	M		Bill	#REF!
4	Cherrie	F			
5	David	M			
6	Euwe	M			
7	Frances	F			
8	Gillian	F			

ix) You obtain "#REF!". This is because the range only has 2 columns, whereas you put in a column number of 3.

1.9 TEXT

a) Function Syntax
=TEXT(value, "format-text")

i)   Value refers to the value to be formatted.

ii) Format text refers to the text format you want to format.

iii) Please note that the format text must be within the double quotation marks.

b) Function Operation

   i)   TEXT function will format the value to the required format.

c) Example

Please see below for the illustration.

	A	B	C
1	Value	TEXT function	Result
2	123	=TEXT(A2,"0")	123
3	123	=TEXT(A3,"0.0")	123.0
4	123	=TEXT(A4,"0.00")	123.00
5	123	=TEXT(A5,"0000")	0123
6	1.23	=TEXT(A6,"0.0%")	123.0%
7	1/4/2016	=TEXT(A6,"d-m")	1-4
8	1/4/2016	=TEXT(A7,"dd-mm")	01-04
9	1/4/2016	=TEXT(A8,"d-mmm")	1-Apr
10	1/4/2016	=TEXT(A9,"d mmmm")	1 April
11	1/4/2016	=TEXT(A10,"d mmm yy")	1 Apr 16
12	1/4/2016	=TEXT(A11,"d mmm yyy")	1 Apr 2016

CHAPTER 2

Query with Grouping Data

2.0 Overview

Query with grouping data is a simple query technique whereby a group of items are pulled upon the given condition. The query is an exact match type and is useful for generating invoice or daily reports.

The technique consists of seven steps namely;

Step 1:- Key in the database in the spreadsheet.
Step 2:- Assign a cell for the condition.
Step 3:- Determine the number of data.
Step 4:- Determine the position of the first data.
Step 5:- Generate the rest of the data.
Step 6:- Extract data to the required range.
Step 7:- Display the extract data to different sheet.

2.1 Extract Invoice data with ONE condition

Step 1:- Key in the database in the spreadsheet.

a) Let's use the database below in range A1:D21 of Sheet1.

	A	B	C	D
1	Inv No	Customer	Qty	Date
2	A0001	April	260	2-Feb
3	A0001	April	250	2-Feb
4	A0002	Billy	177	3-Feb
5	A0002	Billy	156	3-Feb
6	A0002	Billy	133	3-Feb
7	A0003	Cherry	181	4-Feb
8	A0004	Cherry	42	4-Feb
9	A0005	Cherry	114	4-Feb
10	A0005	Cherry	101	4-Feb
11	A0005	Cherry	100	4-Feb
12	A0006	David	207	4-Feb
13	A0007	David	780	4-Feb
14	A0008	Billy	231	4-Feb
15	A0008	Billy	206	4-Feb
16	A0008	Billy	802	4-Feb
17	A0009	David	52	5-Feb
18	A0009	David	56	5-Feb
19	A0009	David	56	5-Feb
20	A0009	David	238	5-Feb
21	A0010	Billy	102	5-Feb

b) Make sure that the data are grouped together according to "Inv No", such as A0001, A0002 and so on.

Step 2:- Assign a cell for the condition.

Assign cell F1 for keying in the condition. For a start, please key in "A0001" in cell F1.

Step 3:- Determine the number of data.

a) Click cell G1.
b) Create a formula in cell G1 as below.
= COUNTIF(A1:A21,F1)

c) Press Enter. Value of cell G1 is 2.
d) This is the count of data related to "A0001".

Step 4:- Determine the row of the first data.

a) Click cell G2.
b) Create a formula in cell G2 as below.
=MATCH(F1,A1:A21,0)
Note that the range in the MATCH function begins from A1, which is including the heading row. It is an exact match.
c) Press Enter. Value of G2 is 2. This is the position of the first data in the range related to "A0001". Thus, the function MATCH acts as a pointer.

Step 5:- Generate the rest of the data.

a) Click cell F2. Type in 1 to denote the first data position (that is in cell G2).
b) Type in 2, 3, 4 and 5 into range F3:F6.
c) Click cell G3.
d) Create a formula in cell G3 as below.
=IF(F3<=$G$1,G2+1,"")
Take note of the absolute cell G1.
e) Copy cell G3 to range G4:G6.
f) You obtain in range F1:G6 as shown below.

	F	G
1	A0001	2
2	1	2
3	2	3
4	3	
5	4	
6	5	

g) For simulation, change cell F1 to "A0009".
h) You obtain in range F1:G6 as shown below.

	F	G
1	A0009	4
2	1	17
3	2	18
4	3	19
5	4	20
6	5	

Step 6:- Extract the data accordingly.

a) Select A1:D1. Click Copy.
b) Click cell H1. Click Paste. You just copied the column heading to another range H1:K1.
c) Click cell H2.
d) Create a formula in cell H2 as below.
   =HLOOKUP(H1,A1:D21,G2,0)
e) Convert the formula to absolute as below.
   =HLOOKUP(H$1,$A$1:$D$21,$G2,0)
f) Notice that for cell H1, we fix only the row, and for cell G2, we fix only the column.
g) Copy cell H2 to range H2:K6.
h) You obtain the following in range F1:K6.

	F	G	H	I	J	K
1	A0009	4	Inv No	Customer	Qty	Date
2	1	17	A0009	David	52	5-Feb
3	2	18	A0009	David	56	5-Feb
4	3	19	A0009	David	56	5-Feb
5	4	20	A0009	David	238	5-Feb
6	5		#REF!	#REF!	#REF!	#REF!

i) Notice that there is an error #REF! in row 6. This is because the cell G6 is blank. So we need to do something.
j) Click cell H2 again.

32

k) Change the formula to as below.
   =IF($G2="","",HLOOKUP(H$1,$A$1:$D$21,$G2,0))
l) The purpose of the IF function is to blank the cell if cell G2 is blank.
m) Copy cell H2 to range H2:K6.
n) You obtain in range F1:K6 as below.

	F	G	H	I	J	K
1	A0009	4	Inv No	Customer	Qty	Date
2	1	17	A0009	David	52	5-Feb
3	2	18	A0009	David	56	5-Feb
4	3	19	A0009	David	56	5-Feb
5	4	20	A0009	David	238	5-Feb
6	5		#REF!	#REF!	#REF!	#REF!

o) Step 3 to step 6 are considered the dummy calculation by the computer.
p) Thus, you can put all these computation in another sheet other than the sheet you wanted to display.

Step 7:- Display the extract data to different sheet.

a) Let's say you perform the dummy computation in Sheet1.
b) In Sheet2, click cell A1.
c) Create a formula in cell A1 as below.
   =Sheet1!H1
d) Copy cell A1 to range A1:D6.
e) Goto Sheet1.
f) Click cell F2.
g) Click Cut.
h) Goto Sheet2.
i) Click cell F1.
j) Press Enter.
k) Change the format accordingly.
l) You obtain the following in range A1:F6.

	A	B	C	D	E	F
1	Inv No	Customer	Qty	Date		A0009
2	A0009	David	52	5-Feb		
3	A0009	David	56	5-Feb		
4	A0009	David	56	5-Feb		
5	A0009	David	238	5-Feb		

m) Notice that Inv No "A0009" has 4 items.

n) For simulation, change cell F1 to "A0008".

o) You obtain the following.

	A	B	C	D	E	F
1	Inv No	Customer	Qty	Date		A0008
2	A0008	Billy	231	4-Feb		
3	A0008	Billy	206	4-Feb		
4	A0008	Billy	802	4-Feb		
5						
6						

p) Notice that Inv No "A0008" has 3 items.

2.2 Extract Output Data with TWO conditions

Step 1:- Key in the database in the spreadsheet.

a) Let's use the database below in range B1:E21 of Sheet1.

	A	B	C	D	E
1		Date	Shift	Machine	Output
2		1-Mar	A	1	1578
3		1-Mar	A	2	1859
4		1-Mar	A	3	1671
5		1-Mar	B	1	1748
6		1-Mar	B	2	1952
7		1-Mar	B	3	1129
8		1-Mar	B	4	1604
9		2-Mar	A	1	1557
10		2-Mar	A	2	1839
11		2-Mar	A	3	1836
12		2-Mar	B	3	1671
13		2-Mar	B	4	1187
14		2-Mar	B	5	1031
15		3-Mar	A	2	1982
16		3-Mar	A	3	1023
17		3-Mar	A	4	1482
18		3-Mar	B	1	1601
19		3-Mar	B	2	1540
20		3-Mar	B	3	1340
21		3-Mar	B	4	1464

b) Make sure that the data are grouped together according to "Date" (column B) and followed by "Shift" (column C).
c) Click cell A2.
d) Create a formula in cell A2 as below.
    = B2&C2
e) Copy cell A2 to range A3: A21.
f) Steps (c) to (e) combine the "Date" and "Shift" into one variable, "date-shift". You obtain the following in range A1:E21.

	A	B	C	D	E
1		Date	Shift	Machine	Output
2	42430A	1-Mar	A	1	1578
3	42430A	1-Mar	A	2	1859
4	42430A	1-Mar	A	3	1671
5	42430B	1-Mar	B	1	1748
6	42430B	1-Mar	B	2	1952
7	42430B	1-Mar	B	3	1129
8	42430B	1-Mar	B	4	1604
9	42431A	2-Mar	A	1	1557
10	42431A	2-Mar	A	2	1839
11	42431A	2-Mar	A	3	1836
12	42431B	2-Mar	B	3	1671
13	42431B	2-Mar	B	4	1187
14	42431B	2-Mar	B	5	1031
15	42432A	3-Mar	A	2	1982
16	42432A	3-Mar	A	3	1023
17	42432A	3-Mar	A	4	1482
18	42432B	3-Mar	B	1	1601
19	42432B	3-Mar	B	2	1540
20	42432B	3-Mar	B	3	1340
21	42432B	3-Mar	B	4	1464

g) Range A2:A21 is just a dummy computation. After you have completed it, you can always hide the column.

Step 2:- Assign a cell for the condition.

a) Assign cell G1 as the condition for Date. Type in 1 Mar.
b) Assign cell G2 as the condition for Shift. Type in "A".
c) Click cell G3.
d) Create a formula in cell G3 as below.
=G1&G2

e) This combines the date and shift into one variable, "date-shift". You obtain the following in range G1:G3.

	G
1	1-Mar
2	A
3	42430A

f) The value 42430 is the date value for 1 March 2016.

Step 3:- Determine the number of data.

a) Click cell I1.
b) Create a formula in cell I1 as below.
=COUNTIF(A1:A21,G3)
c) Press Enter. You obtain value of 3.
d) This is the data count for 1 Mar with shift "A".

Step 4:- Determine the row of the first data.

a) Click cell I2.
b) Create a formula in cell I2 as below.
=MATCH(G3,A1:A21,0)
c) Press Enter. You obtain value of 2.
d) You obtain a result in range G1:I3 as below.

	G	H	I
1	1-Mar		3
2	A		2
3	42430A		

Step 5:- Generate the rest of the data.

a) Click cell H2. Type in 1 to denote the first data.
b) Type in 2, 3, 4 and 5 into range H3:H6.

c) Click cell I3.
d) Create a formula in cell I3 as below.
=IF(H3<=$I$1,I2+1,"")
e) Copy cell I3 to range I4:I6.
f) You obtain the following in range G1:I6.

	G	H	I
1	1-Mar		3
2	A	1	2
3	42430A	2	3
4		3	4
5		4	
6		5	

Step 6:- Extract the data accordingly.

a) Select B1:E1. Click Copy.
b) Click cell J1. Click Paste. You just copied the column heading to another range J1:M1.
c) Click cell J2.
d) Create a formula in cell J2 as below.
=HLOOKUP(J1,B1:E26,I2,0)
e) Convert the formula to absolute as below.
=HLOOKUP(J$1,$B$1:$E$26,$I2,0)
f) Change the formula to as below, for blanking.
=IF($I2="","",HLOOKUP(J$1,$B$1:$E$26,$I2,0))
g) Copy cell J2 to range J2:M6.
h) You obtain the result below in range G1:M6.

38

	G	H	I	J	K	L	M
1	1-Mar		3	Date	Shift	Machine	Output
2	A	1	2	1-Mar	A	1	1578
3	42430A	2	3	1-Mar	A	2	1859
4		3	4	1-Mar	A	3	1671
5		4					
6		5					

Step 7:- Display the extract data to different sheet.

a) Let's say you perform the dummy computation in Sheet1.
b) In Sheet2, click cell A1.
c) Create a formula in cell A1 as below.
   =Sheet1!J1
d) Copy cell A1 to range A1:D6.
e) Goto Sheet1.
f) Click range G1:G2.
g) Click Cut.
h) Goto Sheet2.
i) Click cell F1.
j) Press Enter.
k) You obtain the following in range A1:F6.

	A	B	C	D	E	F
1	Date	Shift	Machine	Output		1-Mar
2	1-Mar	A	1	1578		A
3	1-Mar	A	2	1859		
4	1-Mar	A	3	1671		
5						
6						

l) For simulation, change value of cell F1 to "3-Mar", and the value of cell F2 to B.
m) You obtain the following in range A1:F6.

	A	B	C	D	E	F
1	Date	Shift	Machine	Output		3-Mar
2	3-Mar	B	1	1601		B
3	3-Mar	B	2	1540		
4	3-Mar	B	3	1340		
5	3-Mar	B	4	1464		
6						

2.3 Extract Weekly Data

Step 1:- Key in the database in the spreadsheet.

a)   Let's use the database below in range A1:B21 of Sheet1.

	A	B
1	Date	Output
2	1-Mar	1578
3	2-Mar	1859
4	3-Mar	1671
5	4-Mar	1748
6	5-Mar	1952
7	6-Mar	1129
8	7-Mar	1604
9	8-Mar	1557
10	9-Mar	1839
11	10-Mar	1836
12	11-Mar	1671
13	12-Mar	1187
14	13-Mar	1031
15	14-Mar	1982
16	15-Mar	1023
17	16-Mar	1482
18	17-Mar	1601
19	18-Mar	1540
20	19-Mar	1340
21	20-Mar	1464

b) Make sure the data are in order.
c) Click cell C2.
d) Create a formula in cell C2 as below.
   =WEEKNUM(A2)
e) Copy cell C2 to range C3:C21.
f) You obtain the following in range A1:C21.

	A	B	C
1	Date	Output	
2	1-Mar	1578	10
3	2-Mar	1859	10
4	3-Mar	1671	10
5	4-Mar	1748	10
6	5-Mar	1952	10
7	6-Mar	1129	11
8	7-Mar	1604	11
9	8-Mar	1557	11
10	9-Mar	1839	11
11	10-Mar	1836	11
12	11-Mar	1671	11
13	12-Mar	1187	11
14	13-Mar	1031	12
15	14-Mar	1982	12
16	15-Mar	1023	12
17	16-Mar	1482	12
18	17-Mar	1601	12
19	18-Mar	1540	12
20	19-Mar	1340	12
21	20-Mar	1464	13

Step 2:- Assign a cell for the condition.

Assign cell E1 as the condition for week. Type in 10.

Step 3:- Determine the number of data.

a) Click cell G1.
b) Create a formula in cell G1 as below.
=COUNTIF(C1:C21,E1)
c) Press Enter. Value of cell G1 is 5.
d) This the count of data related to Week 10.

Step 4:- Determine the row of the first data.

   a) Click cell G2.
   b) Create a formula in cell G2 as below.
      =MATCH(E1,C1:C21,0)
   c) Take note that the range in the MATCH function begins from C1, that is including the heading row.
   d) Press Enter. Value of G2 is 2. This is the position of the first data in the range related to Week 10.

Step 5:- Generate the rest of the data.

   a) Type 1 to 7 in range F2:F8.
   b) Create a formula in cell G3 as below.
      =IF(F3<=$G$1,G2+1,"")
      Take note of the absolute cell G1.
   c) Copy cell G3 to range G4:G8.
   d) You obtain the following in range F1:G8.

	F	G
1		5
2	1	2
3	2	3
4	3	4
5	4	5
6	5	6
7	6	
8	7	

Step 6:- Extract the data accordingly.

   a) Select A1:B1. Click Copy.
   b) Click cell H1. Click Paste. You just copied the column heading to another range H1:I1.
   c) Click cell H2.4
   d) Create a formula in cell H2 as below.

=HLOOKUP(H1,A1:B21,G2,0)
e) Convert the formula to absolute as below.
=HLOOKUP(H$1,$A$1:$B$21,$G2,0)
f) Perform blanking for the formula as below.
=IF($G2="","",HLOOKUP(H$1,$A$1:$B$21,$G2,0))
g) Copy cell H2 to range H2:I8.
h) You obtain the following in range E1:I8.

	E	F	G	H	I
1	10		5	Date	Output
2		1	2	1-Mar	1578
3		2	3	2-Mar	1859
4		3	4	3-Mar	1671
5		4	5	4-Mar	1748
6		5	6	5-Mar	1952
7		6			
8		7			

i) For simulation, change the value of cell E1 to 12.
j) You obtain the following in range E1:I8.

	E	F	G	H	I
1	12		7	Date	Output
2		1	14	13-Mar	1031
3		2	15	14-Mar	1982
4		3	16	15-Mar	1023
5		4	17	16-Mar	1482
6		5	18	17-Mar	1601
7		6	19	18-Mar	1540
8		7	20	19-Mar	1340

Step 7:- Display the extract data to different sheet.

a) Let's say you perform the dummy computation in Sheet1.
b) In Sheet2, click cell A1.

c) Create a formula in cell A1 as below.
   =Sheet1!H1
d) Copy cell A1 to range A1:B6.
e) Goto Sheet1.
f) Click range E1.
g) Click Cut.
h) Goto Sheet2.
i) Click cell D1.
j) Press Enter.
k) You obtain the following in range A1:D6.

	A	B	C	D
1	Date	Output		12
2	13-Mar	1031		
3	14-Mar	1982		
4	15-Mar	1023		
5	16-Mar	1482		
6	17-Mar	1601		
7	18-Mar	1540		
8	19-Mar	1340		

l) For simulation, change cell F1 to 13.
m) You obtain the following in range A1:D6.

	A	B	C	D
1	Date	Output		13
2	20-Mar	1464		
3				
4				
5				
6				

CHAPTER 3

Query with Approximate Matching

3.0 Overview

In chapter 2, we learned to pull data when the condition is an exact match. In this chapter, we will learn to pull data when the condition is an approximate match. The concept is quite similar except that the data count method is different.

3.1 Extract daily data with time.

The technique consists of seven steps namely;

> Step 1:-Key in the database in the spreadsheet.
> Step 2:-Assign a cell for the condition.
> Step 3:- Determine the number of data.
> Step 4:- Determine the position of the first data.
> Step 5:- Generate of the rest of the data.
> Step 6:- Extract data to the required range.
> Step 7:- Display extract data to different sheet.

Step 1:- Key in the database in the spreadsheet.
    Let's use the database below in range A1:B21 of Sheet1.

	A	B
1	Date-time	Cycle Time
2	1/3/2016 8:50	231.4
3	1/3/2016 11:13	384.4
4	1/3/2016 14:56	159
5	1/3/2016 17:21	203.6
6	1/3/2016 19:30	197.8
7	3/3/2016 14:12	77.8
8	3/3/2016 15:59	92.6
9	3/3/2016 18:22	62.2
10	3/3/2016 21:31	60.5
11	3/3/2016 23:06	74.2
12	4/3/2016 3:01	63.2
13	4/3/2016 4:33	42.4
14	4/3/2016 6:09	48.9
15	4/3/2016 7:41	29
16	4/3/2016 12:31	90.6
17	4/3/2016 15:46	99.7
18	5/3/2016 2:51	192.1
19	5/3/2016 5:22	385
20	5/3/2016 8:38	105.9
21	5/3/2016 10:48	109.3

Step 2:- Assign a cell for the condition.

a) Assign cell D1 for key-in the condition. For a start, please key-in "1 Mar16" in cell D1.
b) Press Enter. "1-Mar-16" will appear in cell D1.

Step 3:- Determine the number of data.

a) Click cell D2.
b) Create a formula in cell D2 as below.
=MATCH(D1,A2:A21,1)

c) Please note that we use an approximate match instead of exact match.
d) Press Enter. Value of cell D2 is #NA.
e) This is because the first data in the range is 1/3/2016 8:50:47 AM, which is greater than the query condition that is 1/3/2016 0:00 AM. From the range, if counting from row 1, if there is no match for "1-Mar-16", then the value must be 0. Thus, we need to change the formula in cell D2.
f) Convert the formula in cell D2 as below.
   =IFERROR(MATCH(D1,A2:A21,1),0)
g) This formula will always return 0 if found "NA".
h) Press Enter. You obtain value of 0. This indicates no match data.
i) We need to find the last row of the data. Click cell D3.
j) Create a formula in cell D3 as below.
   =MATCH(D1+0.999999,A2:A21,1)
k) Notice that we put the value 0.999999 into the lookup value. This is find the position near to 2/3/2016 23.:59:59. In short, it is the last data of "1-Mar-16".
l) Press Enter. You obtain a value of 5.
m) For testing change the date in cell D1 to "1-Feb-16".
n) Press Enter. You obtain #NA in cell D3.
o) Change the formula in cell D3 to as below.
   =IFERROR(MATCH(D1+0.999999,A2:A21,1),0)
p) Press Enter. You obtain value of 0.
q) Change the date back to "1-Mar-16" in cell D1.
r) The value in cell D2 is 0, and value in cell D3 is 5.
s) Click cell F1.
t) Create a formula in cell F1 as below.
   =D3-D2
u) Press Enter. You obtain value of 5. This indicates the count of 5 data which match approximately with "1-Mar-16".
v) You obtain the following in range D1:F3.

	D	E	F
1	1-Mar-16		5
2	0		
3	5		

Step 4:- Determine the row of the first data.

a) Click cell F2.
b) Create a formula in cell F2 as below.
   = D2+2
c) In actual computation, we should take the value of cell D2 as the first data. But for the step in (b) we put 2. Why?
d) This value 2 comes from 2 values of 1. The first value is that we start with row A2.
e) Change the date in cell D1 to "1-Mar-16".
f) Press Enter. You obtain a value of 2 in cell F2. This is wrong because there is no data. It should be blank.
g) Change the formula in cell F2 to as below.
   =IF(F1=0,"",D2+2)
h) Press Enter. Cell F2 becomes blank.
i) Change the date in cell D1 to "1-Mar-16".
j) You should obtain the following in range D1:F3.

	D	E	F
1	1-Mar-16		5
2	0		2
3	5		

k) Thus, value of cell F2 is the position of the first data.

Step 5:- Generate the rest of the data.

a) Type in 1 to 6 in range E2:E7.
b) Click cell F3.
c) Create a formula in cell F3 as below.
   =IF(E3<=$F$1,F2+1,"")
d) Copy cell F3 to range F4:F7.
e) You obtain the following in range D1:F7.

	D	E	F
1	1-Mar-16		5
2	0	1	2
3	5	2	3
4		3	4
5		4	5
6		5	6
7		6	

Step 6:- Extract the data accordingly.

a) Select A1:B1. Click Copy.
b) Click cell G1. Click Paste. You just copied the column heading to another range G1:H1.
c) Click cell G2.
d) Create a formula in cell G2 as below.
   =HLOOKUP(G1,A1:B23,F2,0)
e) Convert the formula to absolute as below.
   =HLOOKUP(G$1,$A$1:$B$23,$F2,0)
f) Notice that for cell G1, we fix only the row, and for cell F2, we fix only the column.
g) Perform blanking to cell G1, and you obtain the following.
   =IF($F2="","",HLOOKUP(G$1,$A$1:$B$23,$F2,0))
h) Copy cell G2 to range G2:H7.
i) You obtain the following in range D1:H7.

	D	E	F	G	H
1	1-Mar-16		5	Date-time	Cycle Time
2	0	1	2	1/3/2016 8:50	231.4
3	5	2	3	1/3/2016 11:13	384.4
4		3	4	1/3/2016 14:56	159
5		4	5	1/3/2016 17:21	203.6
6		5	6	1/3/2016 19:30	197.8
7		6			

j) For simulation, change the date in cell D1 to "4-Mar-16".
k) You should obtain the following in range D1:H7.

	D	E	F	G	H
1	4-Mar-16		6	Date-time	Cycle Time
2	10	1	12	4/3/2016 3:01	63.2
3	16	2	13	4/3/2016 4:33	42.4
4		3	14	4/3/2016 6:09	48.9
5		4	15	4/3/2016 7:41	29
6		5	16	4/3/2016 12:31	90.6
7		6	17	4/3/2016 14:46	99.7
8		7			

Step 7:- Display the extract data to different sheet.

a) Let's say you perform the dummy computation in Sheet1.
b) In Sheet2, click cell A1.
c) Create a formula in cell A1 as below.
=Sheet1!G1
d) Copy cell A1 to range A1:B7.
e) Go to Sheet1.
f) Click cell D1.
g) Click Cut.
h) Go to Sheet2.
i) Click cell D1.
j) Press Enter.
k) Change the format accordingly.
l) You obtain the following in range A1:D7.

	A	B	C	D
1	Date-time	Cycle Time		4-Mar-16
2	4/3/2016 3:01	63.2		
3	4/3/2016 4:33	42.4		
4	4/3/2016 6:09	48.9		
5	4/3/2016 7:41	29		
6	4/3/2016 12:31	90.6		
7	4/3/2016 14:46	99.7		

m) For simulation, change cell D1 to "3-Mar-16".
n) Change the format accordingly.
o) You obtain the following in range A1:D7.

	A	B	C	D
1	Date-time	Cycle Time		3-Mar-16
2	3/3/2016 14:12	77.8		
3	3/3/2016 15:59	92.6		
4	3/3/2016 18:22	62.2		
5	3/3/2016 21:31	60.5		
6	3/3/2016 23:06	74.2		

3.2 Extract monthly data.

The technique consists of eight steps namely;

Step 1:- Key in the database in the spreadsheet.
Step 2:- Assign a cell for the condition.
Step 3:- Create a table for start date and end date for each month.
Step 4:- Determine the position of the first data.
Step 5:- Determine the number of data.
Step 6:- Generate the rest of the data.
Step 7:- Extract data to the required range.
Step 8:- Display extract data to different sheet.

Step 1:- Key in the database in the spreadsheet.

a) Let's use the database below in range A1:C29 of Sheet1.

	A	B	C
1	Date	Item	Output
2	1-Mar	item1	1795
3	1-Mar	item2	1854
4	2-Mar	item1	1441
5	4-Mar	item1	1101
6	4-Mar	item2	1581
7	5-Mar	item1	1083
8	5-Mar	item2	1337
9	13-Mar	item1	1285
10	15-Mar	item2	1040
11	18-Mar	item1	1380
12	19-Mar	item2	1317
13	22-Mar	item1	1208
14	27-Mar	item2	1007
15	30-Mar	item1	1871
16	1-Apr	item2	1249
17	1-Apr	item1	1679
18	4-Apr	item2	1583
19	5-Apr	item1	1644
20	5-Apr	item2	1111
21	8-Apr	item1	1673
22	10-Apr	item2	1074
23	12-Apr	item1	1509
24	13-Apr	item2	1412
25	19-Apr	item1	1132
26	19-Apr	item2	1919
27	20-Apr	item1	1455
28	20-Apr	item2	1892
29	23-Apr	item1	1947

Step 2:- Assign a cell for the condition.

    a)   Assign cell E1 for keying in the condition. For a start, please key in "Mar16" in cell E1. By doing so, you put in date "1-Mar-16".

    b)   Press Enter. "Mar-16" will appear in cell E1.

Step 3:- Create a table for start date and end date for each month.

    a)   Create table as below in range M1:O13.

	M	N	O
1	Month	Start Date	End Date
2	Jan-16	1-Jan-16	31-Jan-16
3	Feb-16	1-Feb-16	29-Feb-16
4	Mar-16	1-Mar-16	31-Mar-16
5	Apr-16	1-Apr-16	30-Apr-16
6	May-16	1-May-16	31-May-16
7	Jun-16	1-Jun-16	30-Jun-16
8	Jul-16	1-Jul-16	31-Jul-16
9	Aug-16	1-Aug-16	31-Aug-16
10	Sep-16	1-Sep-16	30-Sep-16
11	Oct-16	1-Oct-16	31-Oct-16
12	Nov-16	1-Nov-16	30-Nov-16
13	Dec-16	1-Dec-16	31-Dec-16

Step 4:- Determine the row of the first data.

    a)   Click cell E2.

    b)   Create a formula in cell E2 as below.
        =VLOOKUP(E1,$M$1:$O$13,2)

    c)   Press Enter. You obtain date of "1-Mar-16".

    d)   Click cell E3.

    e)   Create a formula in cell E3 as below.
        =E2+1

f) Copy cell E3 to range E4:E8. Here we use to row 8. If your first data for the month begin with 15th, then you should copy to row 15.

g) You obtain the following in range E1:E8.

	E
1	Mar-16
2	1-Mar
3	2-Mar
4	3-Mar
5	4-Mar
6	5-Mar
7	6-Mar
8	7-Mar

h) Click cell F2.

i) Create a formula in cell F2 as below.
=MATCH(E2,$A$1:$A$29,0)
Note that we use the absolute range.

j) Press Enter. You obtain #NA. This is because there is no date corresponding to"1-Mar-16".

k) To eliminate this error, change the formula to the following.
=IFERROR(MATCH(E2,$A$1:$A$29,0),10000)

l) Press Enter. You obtain 10000. The formula asks the computer to give a value of 10000 if there is a #NA. The value 10000 should correspond to the maximum data in the list.

m) Copy cell F2 to range F3:F8.

n) Click cell F9. Create a formula as below.
=MIN(F2:F8)

o) Press Enter. Value of 2 appeared.

p) This is the first data.

q) You obtain the following in range E1:F9.

🔺	E	F
1	Mar-16	
2	1-Mar	2
3	2-Mar	4
4	3-Mar	10000
5	4-Mar	5
6	5-Mar	7
7	6-Mar	10000
8	7-Mar	10000
9		2

Step 5:- Determine the number of data.

a) Click cell E10.
b) Create a formula in cell E10 as below.
   =VLOOKUP(E1,M1:O13,3)
c) Press Enter. You obtain a date "31-Mar-16".
d) Press cell F10.
e) Create a formula in cell F10 as below.
   =MATCH(E10,A1:A29,1)
f) Press Enter. You obtain a value of 15.
g) This is the row of the last data for month "Mar-16".
h) Click cell H1.
i) Create a formula in cell H1 as below.
   =F10-F9+1
j) Press Enter. You obtain a value of 14. This is the number of data related to month "Mar-16".
k) Thus, you obtain the following in range E1:H10.

⊿	E	F	G	H
1	Mar-16			14
2	1-Mar	2		
3	2-Mar	4		
4	3-Mar	10000		
5	4-Mar	5		
6	5-Mar	7		
7	6-Mar	10000		
8	7-Mar	10000		
9		2		
10	31-Mar	15		

Step 6:- Generate the rest of the data.

a) Type 1 to 15 in range G2:G16.
b) Click cell H2.
c) Create a formula in cell H2 as below.
   =F9
   This is the row of the first data.
d) Click cell H3.
e) Create a formula in cell H3 as below.
   =IF(G3<=$H$1,H2+1,"")
f) Press Enter. You obtain a value of 3 (the row of second data).
g) Copy cell H3 to range H4:H16.
h) You obtain the following in range E1:H16.

	E	F	G	H
1	Mar-16			14
2	1-Mar	2	1	2
3	2-Mar	4	2	3
4	3-Mar	10000	3	4
5	4-Mar	5	4	5
6	5-Mar	7	5	6
7	6-Mar	10000	6	7
8	7-Mar	10000	7	8
9		2	8	9
10	31-Mar	15	9	10
11			10	11
12			11	12
13			12	13
14			13	14
15			14	15
16			15	

i) For simulation, change date in cell E1 to "Apr-16".

j) You should obtain the following in range E1:H16.

	E	F	G	H
1	Apr-16			14
2	1-Apr	16	1	16
3	2-Apr	10000	2	17
4	3-Apr	10000	3	18
5	4-Apr	18	4	19
6	5-Apr	19	5	20
7	6-Apr	10000	6	21
8	7-Apr	10000	7	22
9		16	8	23
10	30-Apr	29	9	24
11			10	25
12			11	26
13			12	27
14			13	28
15			14	29
16			15	

Step 7:- Extract data to the required range.

a) Click range A1:C1.
b) Click copy.
c) Click cell I1. Press Enter.
d) Click cell I2.
e) Create a formula in cell I2 as below.
=HLOOKUP(I1,A1:C29,H2,0)
f) Convert to absolute cells accordingly as below.
=HLOOKUP(I$1,$A$1:$C$29,$H2,0)
g) Change formula to the following, to perform blanking.
=IF(H2="","",HLOOKUP(I$1,$A$1:$C$29,$H2,0))
h) Copy cell I2 to range I2:K16.
i) After performing the necessary formatting, you obtain the following in range I1:K16.

	I	J	K
1	Date	Item	Output
2	1-Apr-16	item2	1249
3	1-Apr-16	item1	1679
4	4-Apr-16	item2	1583
5	5-Apr-16	item1	1644
6	5-Apr-16	item2	1111
7	8-Apr-16	item1	1673
8	10-Apr-16	item2	1074
9	12-Apr-16	item1	1509
10	13-Apr-16	item2	1412
11	19-Apr-16	item1	1132
12	19-Apr-16	item2	1919
13	20-Apr-16	item1	1455
14	20-Apr-16	item2	1892
15	23-Apr-16	item1	1947

Step 8:- Display extract data to different sheet.

a) In Sheet1, select range I1:K6.
b) Click cut.
c) Goto Sheet2.
d) Click cell A1.
e) Press Enter.
f) Goto Sheet1.
g) Click cell E1.
h) Click cut.
i) Goto Sheet2.
j) Click cell E1.
k) Press Enter.
l) You obtain the following in range A1:E16.

	A	B	C	D	E
1	Date	Item	Output		Apr-16
2	1-Apr-16	item2	1249		
3	1-Apr-16	item1	1679		
4	4-Apr-16	item2	1583		
5	5-Apr-16	item1	1644		
6	5-Apr-16	item2	1111		
7	8-Apr-16	item1	1673		
8	10-Apr-16	item2	1074		
9	12-Apr-16	item1	1509		
10	13-Apr-16	item2	1412		
11	19-Apr-16	item1	1132		
12	19-Apr-16	item2	1919		
13	20-Apr-16	item1	1455		
14	20-Apr-16	item2	1892		
15	23-Apr-16	item1	1947		

m) For simulation, change cell E1 to "Mar-16".
n) You obtain the following in range A1:E16.

	A	B	C	D	E
1	Date	Item	Output		Mar-16
2	1-Mar-16	item1	1795		
3	1-Mar-16	item2	1854		
4	2-Mar-16	item1	1441		
5	4-Mar-16	item2	1101		
6	4-Mar-16	item1	1581		
7	5-Mar-16	item2	1083		
8	5-Mar-16	item1	1337		
9	13-Mar-16	item2	1285		
10	15-Mar-16	item1	1040		
11	18-Mar-16	item2	1380		
12	19-Mar-16	item1	1317		
13	22-Mar-16	item2	1208		
14	27-Mar-16	item1	1007		
15	30-Mar-16	item2	1871		

o) Here, I only show you data for two months. In actual practise, you can have more than one year of data. The techniques are the same.

.

CHAPTER 4

Query with Random Data

4.0 Overview

In chapter 2, we performed a query with the data arranged in grouping. If the data is arranged in a random manner, then the technique will fail. That technique is useful because with a big database, we do need a large memory to perform.

In this chapter, we will learn to perform a query when the data is arranged in a random manner.

The technique consists of seven steps namely;

Step 1:- Key in the database in the spreadsheet.
Step 2:- Assign a cell for the condition.
Step 3:- Determine the rows of the required data.
Step 4:- Index the position.
Step 5:- Arrange the position in order.
Step 6:- Extract data to the required range.
Step 7:- Display extract data to different sheet.

4.1 Extract related Invoice No and Sales Quantity for a given item.

Step 1:- Key in the database in the spreadsheet.
Let's use the database below in range A1:C22 of Sheet1.

	A	B	C
1	Invoice	Product	Sales
2	0001	item5	727
3	0002	item2	446
4	0003	item5	607
5	0004	item4	616
6	0005	item2	601
7	0006	item2	271
8	0007	item2	138
9	0008	item3	570
10	0009	item4	810
11	0010	item1	815
12	0011	item5	868
13	0012	item3	136
14	0013	item2	329
15	0014	item3	231
16	0015	item5	412
17	0016	item5	925
18	0017	item4	701
19	0018	item4	674
20	0019	item5	733
21	0020	item1	585
22	0021	item5	557

Step 2:- Assign a cell for the condition.

Assign cell E1 for keying in the condition. For a start, please key-in "item1" in cell E1.

Step 3:- Determine the rows of the required data.

a) Click cell E2.
b) Create a formula in cell E2 as below.
=IF(B2=E1,ROW(B2),"")
c) Put the absolute cell accordingly, as below.
=IF(B2=$E$1,ROW(B2),"")

66

Note that we fixed cell E1 because we need to compare the condition with the list of item in column B.

d) Copy cell E2 to range E3:E22.

e) You should obtain the following for range A1:E22.

	A	B	C	D	E
1	Invoice	Product	Sales		item1
2	0001	item5	727		
3	0002	item2	446		
4	0003	item5	607		
5	0004	item4	616		
6	0005	item2	601		
7	0006	item2	271		
8	0007	item2	138		
9	0008	item3	570		
10	0009	item4	810		
11	0010	item1	815		11
12	0011	item5	868		
13	0012	item3	136		
14	0013	item2	329		
15	0014	item3	231		
16	0015	item5	412		
17	0016	item5	925		
18	0017	item4	701		
19	0018	item4	674		
20	0019	item5	733		
21	0020	item1	585		21
22	0021	item5	557		

f) Now you have found the position of the item1 in the range – that is, row 11 and row 21. Item1 has only 2 data.

g) For simulation, change cell E1 to item5. You should obtain results as below. The position of item5 is row2, row4, row12, row16, row17, row20, and row22. Thus, item5 has 7 data.

	A	B	C	D	E
1	Invoice	Product	Sales		item5
2	0001	item5	727		2
3	0002	item2	446		
4	0003	item5	607		4
5	0004	item4	616		
6	0005	item2	601		
7	0006	item2	271		
8	0007	item2	138		
9	0008	item3	570		
10	0009	item4	810		
11	0010	item1	815		
12	0011	item5	868		12
13	0012	item3	136		
14	0013	item2	329		
15	0014	item3	231		
16	0015	item5	412		16
17	0016	item5	925		17
18	0017	item4	701		
19	0018	item4	674		
20	0019	item5	733		20
21	0020	item1	585		
22	0021	item5	557		22

Step 4:- Index the position.

a) Click cell D2.
b) Create a formula in cell D2 as below.
   =RANK(E2,E2:E22,1)
c) Press Enter. You obtain a value of 1.
d) Put the absolute range accordingly. You obtain as below.
   =RANK(E2,$E$2:$E$22,1)
e) Copy cell D2 to range D3:D22.
f) You should obtain the following for range A1:E22.

	A	B	C	D	E
1	Invoice	Product	Sales		item5
2	0001	item5	727	1	2
3	0002	item2	446	#VALUE!	
4	0003	item5	607	2	4
5	0004	item4	616	#VALUE!	
6	0005	item2	601	#VALUE!	
7	0006	item2	271	#VALUE!	
8	0007	item2	138	#VALUE!	
9	0008	item3	570	#VALUE!	
10	0009	item4	810	#VALUE!	
11	0010	item1	815	#VALUE!	
12	0011	item5	868	3	12
13	0012	item3	136	#VALUE!	
14	0013	item2	329	#VALUE!	
15	0014	item3	231	#VALUE!	
16	0015	item5	412	4	16
17	0016	item5	925	5	17
18	0017	item4	701	#VALUE!	
19	0018	item4	674	#VALUE!	
20	0019	item5	733	6	20
21	0020	item1	585	#VALUE!	
22	0021	item5	557	7	22

g) Notice that you obtain a lot of #VALUE! It is okay; ignore it.
h) Notice that the position of item5 has index starting from 1 to 7, thus 7 items.

Step 5:- Arrange the position in order.

a) Fill in 1 to 10 in range F2:F11.
b) Click cell G2.
c) Create a formula in cell G2 as below.
=VLOOKUP(F2,D2:E22,2,0)
d) Convert to absolute as below.

=VLOOKUP(F2,$D$2:$E$22,2,0)

e) Copy cell G2 to range G3:G11. You obtain the following in range F2:G11.

	F	G
1		
2	1	2
3	2	4
4	3	12
5	4	16
6	5	17
7	6	20
8	7	22
9	8	#N/A
10	9	#N/A
11	10	#N/A

f) Notice that there is an error #NA. This is because there is no index for 8, 9, and 10. Remember, there are only 7 items.

g) Click cell G2. Convert the formula to the following for blanking.
=IFERROR(VLOOKUP(F2,$D$2:$E$22,2,0),"")

h) Copy cell G2 to range G3:G11. You obtain the following in cell F2:G11.

	F	G
1		
2	1	2
3	2	4
4	3	12
5	4	16
6	5	17
7	6	20
8	7	22
9	8	
10	9	
11	10	

i) Notice that the #NA becomes blank.
j) The position in range G2:G11 corresponds to the row number of the item5 as in the list.
k) In this example, we assume that the maximum item for the given condition is 10. This is specify by column F.
l) Notice that all the seven items are arrange in order.

Step 6:- Extract data to the required range.

a) Copy range A1:C1 to range H1:J1.
b) Click cell H2.
c) Create a formula in cell H2 as below.
   =HLOOKUP(H1,A1:C22,G2,0)
d) Convert to absolute as below.
   =HLOOKUP(H$1,$A$1:$C$22,$G2,0)
e) Create blanking for the formula as below.
   =IF($G2="","",HLOOKUP(H$1,$A$1:$C$22,$G2,0))
f) Copy cell H2 to range H2:J11.
g) You should obtain the following for range F2:J11.

	F	G	H	I	J
1			Invoice	Product	Sales
2	1	2	0001	item5	727
3	2	4	0003	item5	607
4	3	12	0011	item5	868
5	4	16	0015	item5	412
6	5	17	0016	item5	925
7	6	20	0019	item5	733
8	7	22	0021	item5	557
9	8				
10	9				
11	10				

h) For simulation, change cell E1 to item2.
i) You should obtain the following for range F1:J11.

	F	G	H	I	J
1			Invoice	Product	Sales
2	1	3	0002	item2	446
3	2	6	0005	item2	601
4	3	7	0006	item2	271
5	4	8	0007	item2	138
6	5	14	0013	item2	329
7	6				
8	7				
9	8				
10	9				
11	10				

Step 7:- Display the extract data to different sheet.

a) Let's say you perform the dummy computation in Sheet1.
b) In Sheet2, click cell A1.
c) Create a formula in cell A1 as below.
   =Sheet1!H1
d) Copy cell A1 to range A1:C11.
e) Goto Sheet1.
f) Click cell E1.
g) Click Cut.
h) Goto Sheet2.
i) Click cell E1.
j) Press Enter.
k) You obtain the following in range A1:E11.

	A	B	C	D	E
1	Invoice	Product	Sales		item2
2	0002	item2	446		
3	0005	item2	601		
4	0006	item2	271		
5	0007	item2	138		
6	0013	item2	329		
7					
8					
9					
10					
11					

l) Notice that item2 has only five items. Therefore, all the data from row 7 to row 11 are blank.

m) For simulation, change cell E1 to item4. You should obtain the following in range A1:E11.

	A	B	C	D	E
1	Invoice	Product	Sales		item4
2	0004	item4	616		
3	0009	item4	810		
4	0017	item4	701		
5	0018	item4	674		
6					
7					
8					
9					
10					
11					

n) Notice that item4 has only 5 items. Therefore, all the data from row 6 to row 11 are blank.

4.2 Extract Maintenance Data with given condition.

In Chapter 2, we have performed query with the data arranged in grouping. If the data is arranged in random manner, then the technique will fail. That technique is useful because with big database, we do need a large memory to perform.

The technique consists of five steps namely;

Step 1:- Key in the database in the spreadsheet.
Step 2:- Assign a cell for the condition.
Step 3:- Determine the rows of the required data.
Step 4:- Extract data to the required range.
Step 5:- Display extract data to different sheet.

Step 1:- Key in the database in the spreadsheet.

a) Let's use the database below in range A1:C23 of Sheet1.

	A	B	C
1	Date	Item	Amount
2	3-Jan	motor	371
3	5-Jan	body	802
4	21-Jan	tyre	765
5	24-Jan	aircond	1440
6	31-Jan	tyre	355
7	2-Feb	aircond	1975
8	20-Feb	body	1493
9	24-Feb	seal	409
10	7-Mar	aircond	159
11	9-Mar	aircond	1233
12	12-Mar	tyre	1533
13	22-Mar	aircond	1640
14	19-Apr	body	308
15	19-Apr	tyre	206
16	23-Apr	tyre	847
17	28-Apr	seal	290
18	30-Apr	seal	1538
19	10-May	aircond	658
20	28-May	body	451
21	31-May	motor	652
22	1-Jun	body	1070
23	5-Jun	aircond	593

Step 2:- Assign a cell for the condition.

Assign cell D1 for keying in the condition. For a start, please key-in "motor" in cell D1.

Step 3:- Determine the rows of the required data.

a) Click cell D2.
b) Create a formula in cell D2 as below.
=COUNTIF(B2:B2,D1)

c) Put the absolute cell accordingly, as below.
=COUNTIF($B$2:B2,$D$1)

d) Note that we fix the first cell of the range $B$2, and we do not fix the second cell B2. We fix cell $D$1 because it is the condition cell.

e) Press Enter. You obtain a value of 1. This refers to the count 1 related to motor.

f) The formula is intended to count the cell that matches with the condition in cell D1 in order, starting from 1.

g) Copy cell D2 to range D3:D23.

h) You obtain the following in range A1:D23.

	A	B	C	D
1	Date	Item	Amount	motor
2	3-Jan	motor	371	1
3	5-Jan	body	802	1
4	21-Jan	tyre	765	1
5	24-Jan	aircond	1440	1
6	31-Jan	tyre	355	1
7	2-Feb	aircond	1975	1
8	20-Feb	body	1493	1
9	24-Feb	seal	409	1
10	7-Mar	aircond	159	1
11	9-Mar	aircond	1233	1
12	12-Mar	tyre	1533	1
13	22-Mar	aircond	1640	1
14	19-Apr	body	308	1
15	19-Apr	tyre	206	1
16	23-Apr	tyre	847	1
17	28-Apr	seal	290	1
18	30-Apr	seal	1538	1
19	10-May	aircond	658	1
20	28-May	body	451	1
21	31-May	motor	652	2
22	1-Jun	body	1070	2
23	5-Jun	aircond	593	2

i) Note that there are two counts related to motor. However, the count 1 repeats downwards until count 2, which then repeats till the last data.
j) We need to eliminate all unrelated item except motor.
k) Click cell D2 again. Change formula to do blanking as below.
=IF(B2=$D$1,COUNTIF($B$2:B2,$D$1),"")
l) The above formula performs blanking if the item in the column does not match the condition in cell D1.
m) Copy cell D2 to range D3:D23.
n) You obtain the following.

	A	B	C	D
1	Date	Item	Amount	motor
2	3-Jan	motor	371	1
3	5-Jan	body	802	
4	21-Jan	tyre	765	
5	24-Jan	aircond	1440	
6	31-Jan	tyre	355	
7	2-Feb	aircond	1975	
8	20-Feb	body	1493	
9	24-Feb	seal	409	
10	7-Mar	aircond	159	
11	9-Mar	aircond	1233	
12	12-Mar	tyre	1533	
13	22-Mar	aircond	1640	
14	19-Apr	body	308	
15	19-Apr	tyre	206	
16	23-Apr	tyre	847	
17	28-Apr	seal	290	
18	30-Apr	seal	1538	
19	10-May	aircond	658	
20	28-May	body	451	
21	31-May	motor	652	2
22	1-Jun	body	1070	
23	5-Jun	aircond	593	

o) Notice that only two items remained, and with the indexing, that is 1 and 2. Thus, we do not need to perform a step for indexing.

Step 4:- Extract related data accordingly.

a) Fill in 1 to 10 in range E2:E11.
b) Copy range A1:C1 to range F1:H1.
c) Click cell F2.
d) Create a formula in cell F2 as below.

78

=INDEX(A2:A23,MATCH(E2,D2:D23,0),0)

e) Notice that we do not use the VLOOKUP function. We make use of INDEX and MATCH to look up the data from right to left.

f) Convert to absolute as below.

=INDEX(A$2:A$23,MATCH(E2,$D$2:$D$23,0),0)

g) Please do not fix column "A".

h) Copy cell F2 to range F3:H11.

i) You obtain the following for range E1:H11.

	E	F	G	H
1		Date	Item	Amount
2	1	42007	motor	371
3	2	42155	motor	652
4	3	#N/A	#N/A	#N/A
5	4	#N/A	#N/A	#N/A
6	5	#N/A	#N/A	#N/A
7	6	#N/A	#N/A	#N/A
8	7	#N/A	#N/A	#N/A
9	8	#N/A	#N/A	#N/A
10	9	#N/A	#N/A	#N/A
11	10	#N/A	#N/A	#N/A

j) Please note that there are two items. The extracted data for row 3 onwards is #NA. This is because we do not perform blanking yet.

k) Click cell F2.

l) Create a formula as below for blanking.

=IFERROR(INDEX(A$2:A$23,MATCH(E2,$D$2:$D$23,0),0),"")

m) Performed the necessary formatting.

n) You obtain the following in range E1:H11.

⊿	E	F	G	H
1		Date	Item	Amount
2	1	3-Jan	motor	371
3	2	31-May	motor	652
4	3			
5	4			
6	5			
7	6			
8	7			
9	8			
10	9			
11	10			

o) For simulation, click cell D1. Change to "aircond".
p) Press Enter. You obtain the following in range E1:H11.

⊿	E	F	G	H
1		Date	Item	Amount
2	1	24-Jan	aircond	1440
3	2	2-Feb	aircond	1975
4	3	7-Mar	aircond	159
5	4	9-Mar	aircond	1233
6	5	22-Mar	aircond	1640
7	6	10-May	aircond	658
8	7	5-Jun	aircond	593
9	8			
10	9			
11	10			

Step 5:- Display the extract data to different sheet.

a) Let's say you perform the dummy computation in Sheet1.
b) In Sheet2, click cell A1.
c) Create a formula in cell A1 as below.
=Sheet1!F1

d) Copy cell A1 to range A1:C11.
e) Goto Sheet1.
f) Click cell D1.
g) Click Cut.
h) Goto Sheet2.
i) Click cell E1.
j) Press Enter.
k) You obtain the following in range A1:E11.

	A	B	C	D	E
1	Date	Item	Amount		aircond
2	Jan-15	aircond	1440		
3	Feb-15	aircond	1975		
4	Mar-15	aircond	159		
5	Mar-15	aircond	1233		
6	Mar-15	aircond	1640		
7	May-15	aircond	658		
8	Jun-15	aircond	593		
9					
10					
11					

l) For simulation, change the value of cell E1 to "tyre".
m) You obtain the following in range A1:E11.

	A	B	C	D	E
1	Date	Item	Amount		tyre
2	Jan-15	tyre	765		
3	Jan-15	tyre	355		
4	Mar-15	tyre	1533		
5	Apr-15	tyre	206		
6	Apr-15	tyre	847		
7					
8					
9					
10					
11					

CHAPTER 5

Query with Two Conditions

5.0 Overview

In chapter 4, we have seen query with only one condition. Sometimes we encountered more than one condition. In this chapter, we will learn how to perform query on 2 conditions. And the technique is applicable to multiple conditions.

5.1 Extract related DO No for the given item and Sales No.

The technique consists of eight steps namely;

> Step 1:- Key in the database in the spreadsheet.
> Step 2:- Transform the data into unique data.
> Step 3:- Assign a cell for the condition.
> Step 4:- Determine the rows of the required data.
> Step 5:- Index the position.
> Step 6:- Arrange the position in order.
> Step 7:- Extract data to the required range.
> Step 8:- Display extract data to different sheet.

Step 1:- Key in the database in the spreadsheet.
    Let's use the database below in range A1:C24 of Sheet1.

	A	B	C
1	DO No	Item	Sales No
2	30001	item7	10001
3	30001	item6	10003
4	30001	item3	10002
5	30001	item4	10004
6	30002	item6	10001
7	30002	item7	10001
8	30002	item2	10002
9	30002	item3	10002
10	30002	item7	10002
11	30003	item7	10004
12	30004	item5	10001
13	30004	item2	10004
14	30005	item5	10003
15	30005	item3	10002
16	30006	item1	10002
17	30006	item7	10001
18	30006	item2	10001
19	30007	item4	10003
20	30008	item5	10003
21	30009	item5	10004
22	30009	item3	10002
23	30010	item5	10005
24	30010	item5	10002

Step 2:- Transform the data into unique data.

a) Click cell D2.
b) Create a formula in cell D2 as below.
   =C2&B2
c) Press Enter. You obtain value of 10001item7.
d) Copy cell D2 to range D3:D24.
e) You should obtain the following for range A1:D24.

84

	A	B	C	D
1	DO No	Item	Sales No	
2	30001	item7	10001	10001item7
3	30001	item6	10003	10003item6
4	30001	item3	10002	10002item3
5	30001	item4	10004	10004item4
6	30002	item6	10001	10001item6
7	30002	item7	10001	10001item7
8	30002	item2	10002	10002item2
9	30002	item3	10002	10002item3
10	30002	item7	10002	10002item7
11	30003	item7	10004	10004item7
12	30004	item5	10001	10001item5
13	30004	item2	10004	10004item2
14	30005	item5	10003	10003item5
15	30005	item3	10002	10002item3
16	30006	item1	10002	10002item1
17	30006	item7	10001	10001item7
18	30006	item2	10001	10001item2
19	30007	item4	10003	10003item4
20	30008	item5	10003	10003item5
21	30009	item5	10004	10004item5
22	30009	item3	10002	10002item3
23	30010	item5	10005	10005item5
24	30010	item5	10002	10002item5

f) Column "F" is the unique data for Sales No & Item.

g) Thus, the query condition must be based on column "F".

Step 3:- Assign a cell for the condition.

a) Assign cell F1 as a condition for Item. For a start, type "item7" in cell F1.

b) Assign cell G1 as a condition for Sales No. For a start, type "10001" in cell G1.
c) Click cell E1.
d) Create a formula in cell E1 as below.
=G1&F1
e) Press Enter. You obtain 10001item7 in cell E1.
f) Now we have transformed the conditions of Sales No. and Item to become one condition – that is, "Sales No. - Item", a unique condition.
g) Thus, cell E1 is the assigned cell for condition, a combination of Sales No. and Item.

Step 4:- Define the positions of all the related items.

a) Click cell F2.
b) Create a formula in cell F2 as below.
=IF(D2=E1,ROW(D2),"")
c) Put the absolute cell accordingly, as below.
=IF(D2=$E$1,ROW(D2),"")
d) Note that we fix cell E1 because we need to compare the condition with the list of item in column D.
e) Press Enter. You obtain a value of 2.
f) Copy cell F2 to range F3:F24.
g) You should obtain the following for range D1:G24.

	D	E	F	G
1		10001item7	item7	10001
2	10001item7		2	
3	10003item6			
4	10002item3			
5	10004item4			
6	10001item6			
7	10001item7		7	
8	10002item2			
9	10002item3			
10	10002item7			
11	10004item7			
12	10001item5			
13	10004item2			
14	10003item5			
15	10002item3			
16	10002item1			
17	10001item7		17	
18	10001item2			
19	10003item4			
20	10003item5			
21	10004item5			
22	10002item3			
23	10005item5			
24	10002item5			

h) Now you have to find the position of the Sales No. 10001 with item7 in the range, which are rows 2, 7, and 17.

Step 5:- Index the position.

a) Click cell E2.
b) Create a formula in cell E2 as below.
   =RANK(F2,F2:F24,1)

c) Press Enter. You obtain a value of 1.
d) Put the absolute range accordingly. You obtain the following.
=RANK(F2,$F$2:$F$24,1)
e) Copy cell E2 to range E3:E24.
f) You should obtain the following for range D1:G24.

	D	E	F	G
1		10001item7	item7	10001
2	10001item7	1	2	
3	10003item6	#VALUE!		
4	10002item3	#VALUE!		
5	10004item4	#VALUE!		
6	10001item6	#VALUE!		
7	10001item7	2	7	
8	10002item2	#VALUE!		
9	10002item3	#VALUE!		
10	10002item7	#VALUE!		
11	10004item7	#VALUE!		
12	10001item5	#VALUE!		
13	10004item2	#VALUE!		
14	10003item5	#VALUE!		
15	10002item3	#VALUE!		
16	10002item1	#VALUE!		
17	10001item7	3	17	
18	10001item2	#VALUE!		
19	10003item4	#VALUE!		
20	10003item5	#VALUE!		
21	10004item5	#VALUE!		
22	10002item3	#VALUE!		
23	10005item5	#VALUE!		
24	10002item5	#VALUE!		

g) You will obtain a lot of #VALUE! It is okay; ignore it.

h) Notice that the position of 10001item7 has index starting from 1 to 3, and thus there are 3 items.

Step 6:- Arrange the position in order.

a) Fill in 1 to 10 in range G2:G11.
b) Click cell H2.
c) Create a formula in cell H2 as below.
=VLOOKUP(G2,E2:F24,2,0)
d) Convert to absolute as below.
=VLOOKUP(G2,$E$2:$F$24,2,0)
e) Copy cell H2 to range H3:H11. You obtain the following in range G1:H11.

	G	H
1	10001	
2	1	2
3	2	7
4	3	17
5	4	#N/A
6	5	#N/A
7	6	#N/A
8	7	#N/A
9	8	#N/A
10	9	#N/A
11	10	#N/A

f) Notice that there is an error #NA. This is because there is no index for 4 to 10. Remember, there are only three items.
g) Click cell H2. Convert the formula to as below for blanking.
=IFERROR(VLOOKUP(G2,$E$2:$F$24,2,0),"")
h) Copy cell H2 to range H3:H11. You obtain the following in range G2:H11.

	G	H
1	10001	
2	1	2
3	2	7
4	3	17
5	4	
6	5	
7	6	
8	7	
9	8	
10	9	
11	10	

i) Notice that the #NA becomes blank.

Step 7:- Extract the required data accordingly.

a) Copy range A1:C1 to range I1:K1.
b) Click cell I2.
c) Create a formula in cell I2 as below.
   =HLOOKUP(I1,A1:C24,H2,0)
d) Convert to absolute as below.
   =HLOOKUP(I$1,$A$1:$C$24,$H2,0)
e) Create blanking for the formula as below.
   =IFERROR(HLOOKUP(I$1,$A$1:$C$24,$H2,0),"")
f) Copy cell I2 to range I2:K11.
g) You should obtain the following for range G1:K11.

	G	H	I	J	K
1	10001		DO No	Item	Sales No
2	1	2	30001	item7	10001
3	2	7	30002	item7	10001
4	3	17	30006	item7	10001
5	4				
6	5				
7	6				
8	7				
9	8				
10	9				
11	10				

h) Thus, we already extract the related DO No., which are 30001, 30002, and 30006, related to the given conditions – that is, "10001" and "item7".

i) For simulation, change the value of F1 to "item3", and the value of G1 to "10002".

j) You should obtain the following for range G1:K11.

	G	H	I	J	K
1	10002		DO No	Item	Sales No
2	1	4	30001	item3	10002
3	2	9	30002	item3	10002
4	3	15	30005	item3	10002
5	4	22	30009	item3	10002
6	5				
7	6				
8	7				
9	8				
10	9				
11	10				

Step 8:- Display the extract data to different sheet.

a) Let's say you perform the dummy computation in Sheet1.
b) In Sheet2, click cell A1.
c) Create a formula in cell A1 as below.
   =Sheet1!I1
d) Copy cell A1 to range A1:C11.
e) Goto Sheet1.
f) Click cell F1.
g) Click Cut.
h) Goto Sheet2.
i) Click cell E1.
j) Press Enter.
k) Goto Sheet1.
l) Click cell G1.
m) Click Cut.
n) Goto Sheet2.
o) Click cell E2.
p) Press Enter.
q) You obtain the following in range A1:E11.

	A	B	C	D	E
1	DO No	Item	Sales No		item3
2	30001	item3	10002		10002
3	30002	item3	10002		
4	30005	item3	10002		
5	30009	item3	10002		
6					
7					
8					
9					
10					
11					

r) Notice that there are four items. Therefore, all the data from row 6 to row 11 are blank.

s) For simulation, change cell E1 to "item5", and cell E2 to "10004".
t) You obtain the following in range A1:E11.

	A	B	C	D	E
1	DO No	Item	Sales No		item5
2	30009	item5	10004		10004
3					
4					
5					
6					
7					
8					
9					
10					
11					

5.2 Extract data with ONE or TWO conditions

The above technique shows us how to extract data when we meet with exactly two conditions. In this section, we will see how to perform a query when we have one condition, both, or none.

The technique is similar to how we perform the filter method provided by Excel. However, with this technique, once filtering, you can still use the extracted data as a new database. With this, you can do other Excel operation as per normal. And with this technique, the filtered data can be used as a report in a selected range.

The technique is quite similar to the above technique, but the difference lies in steps 2 and 3.

The technique consists of eight steps namely;

Step 1:- Key in the database in the spreadsheet.
Step 2:- Assign a cell for the condition.
Step 3:- Transform the data into unique data.
Step 4:- Determine the rows of the required data.
Step 5:- Index the position.

Step 6:- Arrange the position in order.
Step 7:- Extract data to the required range.
Step 8:- Display extract data to different sheet.

Step 1:- Key in the database in the spreadsheet.
Let's use the database below in range A1:C26 of Sheet1.

	A	B	C
1	T	W	m3
2	22.0	33.0	0.4637
3	39.0	46.0	1.0234
4	39.0	46.0	1.8389
5	39.0	46.0	1.7589
6	27.2	51.8	0.2558
7	36.0	50.5	0.6396
8	36.5	50.5	0.3998
9	36.5	50.5	1.7589
10	37.0	44.0	0.1119
11	22.5	83.0	0.2079
12	22.0	44.0	0.3198
13	22.0	44.0	0.1439
14	36.0	50.5	0.3038
15	36.0	50.5	0.5756
16	36.0	50.5	0.1759
17	33.5	46.5	0.2718
18	39.0	46.0	0.6396
19	22.0	43.0	0.0352
20	20.0	46.5	0.1279
21	22.0	67.0	0.1407
22	22.0	67.0	0.0704
23	24.0	70.0	1.8389
24	22.0	43.0	0.2079
25	22.0	43.0	0.0704
26	36.5	44.0	0.1599

Step 2:- Assign a cell for the condition.

a) Assign cell F1 as condition for T. For a start, key in 22.0.
b) Assign cell G1 as condition for W. For a start, key in 44.0.
c) Click cell E1.
d) Create a formula in cell E1 as below.
   =IF(F1="","",F1)&IF(G1="","",G1)
e) We are trying to make the condition flexible. If we do not key in cell F1, then the condition means any value of T in cell F1 is considered. This is similar to any value of W in cell G1.
f) Press Enter. You obtain a value of 2244. This is a combination of 22 and 44. (This is without formatting)
g) You should obtain the following for range E1:G1.

	E	F	G
1	2244	22.0	44.0
2			

h) Notice that in cell E1, the value is 2244; that is T and W combined together.
i) Now cell E1 becomes the condition for both T and W.

Step 3:- Transform the data into unique data.

a) Click cell D2.
b) Create a formula in cell D2 as below.
   =IF(F1="","",A2)&IF(G1="","",B2)
c) Press Enter. You obtain value of 2233.
d) Because cells F1 and G1 are the conditions, it must be transformed to be an absolute cell before it's copied downwards. Convert the formula to absolute.
   =IF($F$1="","",A2)&IF($G$1="","",B2)
e) Copy cell D2 to range D3:D26.
f) You should obtain the following for range A1:D26.

	A	B	C	D
1	T	W	m3	
2	22.0	33.0	0.4637	2233
3	39.0	46.0	1.0234	3946
4	39.0	46.0	1.8389	3946
5	39.0	46.0	1.7589	3946
6	27.2	51.8	0.2558	27.251.8
7	36.0	50.5	0.6396	3650.5
8	36.5	50.5	0.3998	36.550.5
9	36.5	50.5	1.7589	36.550.5
10	37.0	44.0	0.1119	3744
11	22.5	83.0	0.2079	22.583
12	22.0	44.0	0.3198	2244
13	22.0	44.0	0.1439	2244
14	36.0	50.5	0.3038	3650.5
15	36.0	50.5	0.5756	3650.5
16	36.0	50.5	0.1759	3650.5
17	33.5	46.5	0.2718	33.546.5
18	39.0	46.0	0.6396	3946
19	22.0	43.0	0.0352	2243
20	20.0	46.5	0.1279	2046.5
21	22.0	67.0	0.1407	2267
22	22.0	67.0	0.0704	2267
23	24.0	70.0	1.8389	2470
24	22.0	43.0	0.2079	2243
25	22.0	43.0	0.0704	2243
26	36.5	44.0	0.1599	36.544

g) Note that in column D, we obtain data such as 27.251.8. This is okay because it combines the value of T and W.

h) Thus, Column D will be the unique range list as correspond to the unique condition in cell E1.

Step 4:- Determine the rows of the required data.

    a) Click cell F2.
    b) Create a formula in cell F2 as below.
       =IF(D2=E1,ROW(D2),"")
    c) Put the absolute cell accordingly, as below.
       =IF(D2=$E$1,ROW(D2),"")
    d) Press Enter. You obtain blank.
    e) Note that we fix cell E1 because we need to compare the condition with the list of item in column D.
    f) Copy cell F2 to range F3:F26.
    g) You should obtain the following for range D1:G26.

	D	E	F	G
1		2244	22.0	44.0
2	2233			
3	3946			
4	3946			
5	3946			
6	27.251.8			
7	3650.5			
8	36.550.5			
9	36.550.5			
10	3744			
11	22.583			
12	2244		12	
13	2244		13	
14	3650.5			
15	3650.5			
16	3650.5			
17	33.546.5			
18	3946			
19	2243			
20	2046.5			
21	2267			
22	2267			
23	2470			
24	2243			
25	2243			
26	36.544			

h) Now you have find the position of the T = 22.0 and W = 44.0 in the range, which are rows 12 and 13.

98

Step 5:- Index the position.

a) Click cell E2.
b) Create a formula in cell E2 as below.
=RANK(F2,F2:F26,1)
c) Press Enter. You obtain #VALUE!.
d) Put the absolute range accordingly. You obtain the following.
=RANK(F2,$F$2:$F$26,1)
e) Copy cell E2 to range E3:E26.
f) You should obtain the following for range D1:G26.

	D	E	F	G
1		2244	22.0	44.0
2	2233	#VALUE!		
3	3946	#VALUE!		
4	3946	#VALUE!		
5	3946	#VALUE!		
6	27.251.8	#VALUE!		
7	3650.5	#VALUE!		
8	36.550.5	#VALUE!		
9	36.550.5	#VALUE!		
10	3744	#VALUE!		
11	22.583	#VALUE!		
12	2244	1	12	
13	2244	2	13	
14	3650.5	#VALUE!		
15	3650.5	#VALUE!		
16	3650.5	#VALUE!		
17	33.546.5	#VALUE!		
18	3946	#VALUE!		
19	2243	#VALUE!		
20	2046.5	#VALUE!		
21	2267	#VALUE!		
22	2267	#VALUE!		
23	2470	#VALUE!		
24	2243	#VALUE!		
25	2243	#VALUE!		
26	36.544	#VALUE!		

g) You will obtain a lot of #VALUE! It is okay; ignore it.

h) Notice that the position of 12 and 13 has indexing starting from 1 and 2, and thus there are two items.

Step 6:- Arrange the position in order.

a) Fill in 1 to 10 in range G2:G11.
b) Click cell H2.
c) Create a formula in cell H2 as below.
   =VLOOKUP(G2,E2:F26,2,0)
d) Convert to absolute as below.
   =VLOOKUP(G2,$E$2:$F$26,2,0)
e) Click cell H2. Convert the formula to the following for blanking.
   =IFERROR(VLOOKUP(G2,$E$2:$F$26,2,0),"")
f) Copy cell H2 to range H3:H11. You obtain the following in range G2:H11.

	G	H
1	44.0	
2	1	12
3	2	13
4	3	
5	4	
6	5	
7	6	
8	7	
9	8	
10	9	
11	10	

Step 7:- Extract the required data accordingly.

a) Copy range A1:C1 to range I1:K1.
b) Click cell I2.
c) Create a formula in cell I2 as below.
   =HLOOKUP(I1,A1:C26,H2,0)
d) Convert to absolute as below.
   =HLOOKUP(I$1,$A$1:$C$26,$H2,0)
e) Create blanking for the formula as below.

=IFERROR(HLOOKUP(I$1,$A$1:$C$26,$H2,0),"")

f) Copy cell I2 to range I2:K11.
g) You should obtain the following for range G1:K11.

	G	H	I	J	K
1	44.0		T	W	m3
2	1	12	22	44	0.3198
3	2	13	22	44	0.1439
4	3				
5	4				
6	5				
7	6				
8	7				
9	8				
10	9				
11	10				

h) For simulation, delete the value in cell G1. You should obtain the following in range G1:K11.

	G	H	I	J	K
1			T	W	m3
2	1	2	22	33	0.4637
3	2	12	22	44	0.3198
4	3	13	22	44	0.1439
5	4	19	22	43	0.0352
6	5	21	22	67	0.1407
7	6	22	22	67	0.0704
8	7	24	22	43	0.2079
9	8	25	22	43	0.0704
10	9				
11	10				

i) Notice that the value T is 22.0, whereas there are few values of W.

j) Delete cell F1, and key-in W = 44.0 in cell G1. You should obtain the following in range G1:K11.

	G	H	I	J	K
1	44.0		T	W	m3
2	1	10	37	44	0.1119
3	2	12	22	44	0.3198
4	3	13	22	44	0.1439
5	4	26	36.5	44	0.1599
6	5				
7	6				
8	7				
9	8				
10	9				
11	10				

k) Notice that the value W is 44.0, whereas there are few values of T.
l) Delete the value in both cell F1 and G1. You should obtain the following in range G1:K11.

	G	H	I	J	K
1			T	W	m3
2	1	2	22	33	0.4637
3	2	3	39	46	1.0234
4	3	4	39	46	1.8389
5	4	5	39	46	1.7589
6	5	6	27.2	51.8	0.2558
7	6	7	36	50.5	0.6396
8	7	8	36.5	50.5	0.3998
9	8	9	36.5	50.5	1.7589
10	9	10	37	44	0.1119
11	10	11	22.5	83	0.2079

m) In this case, you are extracting all the values from the range. With 10 rows, it is not sufficient. Thus, you need to increase the row.

n) Key-in 36.0 into cell F1, and 50.5 into cell G1.
o) You obtain the following in range G1:K11.

	G	H	I	J	K
1	50.5		T	W	m3
2	1	7	36	50.5	0.6396
3	2	14	36	50.5	0.3038
4	3	15	36	50.5	0.5756
5	4	16	36	50.5	0.1759
6	5				
7	6				
8	7				
9	8				
10	9				
11	10				
12					

Step 8:- Display the extract data to different sheet.

a) Let's say you perform the dummy computation in Sheet1.
b) In Sheet2, click cell A1.
c) Create a formula in cell A1 as below.
   =Sheet1!I1
d) Copy cell A1 to range A1:C11.
e) Goto Sheet1.
f) Click cell F1.
g) Click Cut.
h) Goto Sheet2.
i) Click cell E1.
j) Press Enter.
k) Goto Sheet1.
l) Click cell G1.
m) Click Cut.
n) Goto Sheet2.
o) Click cell E2.

p) Press Enter.

q) You obtain the following in range A1:E11.

	A	B	C	D	E
1	T	W	m3		36.0
2	36	50.5	0.6396		50.5
3	36	50.5	0.3038		
4	36	50.5	0.5756		
5	36	50.5	0.1759		
6					
7					
8					
9					
10					
11					

r) For simulation, change the value T = 39.0 and W = 46.0 in cells E1 and E2, respectively. You should obtain the following in range A1:E11.

	A	B	C	D	E
1	T	W	m3		39.0
2	39	46	1.0234		46.0
3	39	46	1.8389		
4	39	46	1.7589		
5	39	46	0.6396		
6					
7					
8					
9					
10					
11					

CHAPTER 6

Dynamic Text

6.0 Overview

In normal practise, we will put heading notes and remarks below for a report. Whenever the conditions or the value change we will manually change these notes or remarks. Sometimes, we tend to forget.

This problem can be solved if we make use of dynamic text. What is dynamic text? Dynamic text is a text that change automatically with the given condition.

6.1 Dynamic text in ROI computation

The technique consists of three steps namely;

Step 1:- Create an investment data table.
Step 2:- Create ROI calculation step.
Step 3:- Convert the Step 2 to dynamic text.

Step 1:- Key in the database in the spreadsheet.
Let's use the data as below in range A1:C6.

	A	B	C
1	ROI Calulation		
2			
3	Investment Value:	$50,000.00	
4	Manpower Saving	20	persons
5	Saving / person	$1,000.00	per month
6	Total Saving	$20,000.00	per month

Step 2:- Create ROI calculation step.

a) If we will to use simple ROI calculation, it should be as below in range A1:C11.

	A	B	C
1	ROI Calculation		
2			
3	Investment Value	$50,000.00	
4	Manpower Saving	20	persons
5	Saving / person	$1,000.00	per month
6	Total Saving	$20,000.00	per month
7			
8			
9	ROI =	Investment / Total Saving	
10		50000 / 20000	
11		2.5	months

b) In cell B10, we type manually 50000 / 20000. If we change the investment value to 60000, then we have to retype the term to 60000 / 20000. Similarly, if we to change the total savings to 25000, then we have to retype the term: 50000 / 25000. This will be done manually. The disadvantages are that we need extra time and might forget to change the note.

c) Similarly, in cell B11, we create the following formula.
=B3/B6

d) Of course, the value in cell B11 will change automatically. Only the cell B10 will not change automatically.

Step 3:- Convert the Step 2 to dynamic text.

a) In this example, we simply need to put a formula in cell B10.

b) Create a formula in cell B10.
=B3&" / "&B6

c) The formula consists of three terms joined by the ampersand sign, &.

d) The first tem is cell B3. This refers to the investment value. In this case, it is 50000.

e) The second term is "/". This is a text term, so it should be within the double quotation marks.

f) The third term is cell B6. This refers to the total savings value. In this case, it is 20000.

g) You obtain the following in range A1:C11.

	A	B	C
1	ROI Calculation		
2			
3	Investment Value	$50,000.00	
4	Manpower Saving	20	persons
5	Saving / person	$1,000.00	per month
6	Total Saving	$20,000.00	per month
7			
8			
9	ROI =	Investment / Total Saving	
10		50000 / 20000	
11		2.5	months

h) It is the same because we type it in manually. But the difference is that there is a formula in cell B10 for dynamic text.

6.2 Dynamic text link with formula

The technique consists of three steps namely;

Step 1:- Create a table.
Step 2:- Create simple query.
Step 3:- Convert the Step 2 to dynamic text.

Step 1:- Create a table as below in range A1:C7.

	A	B	C
1	Name	Sex	Age
2	April	F	37
3	Bill	M	33
4	Cherrie	F	42
5	David	M	32
6	Euwe	M	40
7	Frances	F	28

Step 2:- Create simple query

a) Copy headings range A1:C1 to range A9:C9.
b) Key in "Euwe" in cell A10.
c) Create a formula in cell B10 as below.
=VLOOKUP(A10,A2:C7,2,0)
d) Create a formula in cell C10 as below.
=VLOOKUP(A10,A2:C7,3,0)
e) You obtain the following in range A1:C10.

	A	B	C
1	Name	Sex	Age
2	April	F	37
3	Bill	M	33
4	Cherrie	F	42
5	David	M	32
6	Euwe	M	40
7	Frances	F	28
8			
9	Name	Sex	Age
10	Euwe	M	40

f) We can write a remark as below.
Euwe is a man age 40.

g) If we change the value in cell A10 to "David", we obtain the following in range A9:A10.

	A	B	C
9	Name	Sex	Age
10	David	M	32

h) Then, we have to change the remark to as below.
David is a man age 32.

i) This will be a tedious work.

Step 3:- Convert the Step 2 to dynamic text.

a) Create a formula in cell A13 as below.
=A10

b) Change the formula in (a) to as below.
=A10&" is a"

c) Change the formula in (b) to as below.
=A10&" is a "&B10

d) Change the formula in (c) to as below.
=A10&" is a "&B10&" age"

e) Change the formula in (d) to as below.
   =A10&" is a "&B10&" age "&C10
f) Change the formula in (e) to as below.
   =A10&" is a "&B10&" age "&C10&"."
g) You obtain the following in range A9:C13.

	A	B	C
9	Name	Sex	Age
10	David	M	32
11			
12			
13	David is a M age 32.		

h) Notice that you obtain the following in cell A13.
   David is a M age 32.
i) We have to change the term "M" to "man".
j) Change the formula in cell A13 to as below.
   =A10&" is a "&IF(B10="M","man","lady")&" age "&C10&"."
k) Notice that we make use of the Excel formula just after the ampersand sign without a break.
l) In short, we can use any Excel formula just after the ampersand sign without a break.
m) Now the cell A13 becomes a dynamic text.
n) For simulation, change the value of A10 to "April".
o) You obtain the following in range A9:C13.

	A	B	C
9	Name	Sex	Age
10	April	F	37
11			
12			
13	April is a lady age 37.		

p) The dynamic text in cell A13 can still be improved to as below.
q) Change the formula in cell A13 as below.

=A10&" is a "&IF(VLOOKUP(A10,A2:C7,2,0)="M","man","l
ady")&" age "&C10&"."

r) We add VLOOKUP function in place of cell B10. This is because cell
B10 has this VLOOKUP formula.

s) Similarly, we can change the above formula to the following for
cell C10.
=A10&" is a "&IF(VLOOKUP(A10,A2:C7,2,0)="M","man","l
ady")&" age "&VLOOKUP(A10,A2:C7,3,0)&"."

t) Thus, the formula in cell A13 only depends on the condition in cell
A10 and range A2:C7.

u) Lastly for simulation, change cell A10 to "Bill".

v) You obtain the following in range A9:C13.

	A	B	C
9	Name	Sex	Age
10	Bill	M	33
11			
12			
13	Bill is a man age 33.		

6.3 Dynamic text for report title 1

In normal practice, we usually put up the title for a half-monthly summary
table as follows.

Wages for period 01–15 April 2016
Or
Wages for period 16–30 April 2016

In normal practice, this is done manually. If we use query to extract the
data based on the month or period, then we might forget to change the title.
With dynamic text, the title will change according to the query parameters.

The technique consists of two steps namely;

Step 1:- Assign the start date and end date.
Step 2:- Convert to dynamic text.

Step 1:- Assign the start date and end date.

a) Assign cell A1 as start date. As a start, key in "1-Apr-16".
b) Assign cell A2 as end date. As a start, key in "15-Apr-16".

Step 2:- Convert to dynamic text.

a) Click cell A4.
b) Create a formula in cell A4 as below.
   ="Wages for period:-"
c) Change the formula in (b) to as below.
   ="Wages for period:- "&A1
d) Press Enter. You obtain the following in range A1:A4.

	A
1	1-Apr-16
2	15-Apr-16
3	
4	Wages for period:- 42461

e) Notice that cell A4 has a term 42461. Actually, this is the date value for "1-Apr-16". Ignore it.
f) Change the formula in (c) to the following.
   ="Wages for period:- "&TEXT(A1,"dd")
g) Press Enter. You obtain the following in range A1:A4.

	A
1	1-Apr-16
2	15-Apr-16
3	
4	Wages for period:- 01

h) Notice that cell A4 term 42461 has changed to 01. Actually, the TEXT function only pulls the day term from the date "1-Apr-16".
i) Change the formula in (f) to as below.
   ="Wages for period:- "&TEXT(A1,"dd")&" -"

114

j) Change the formula in (i) to as below.

="Wages for period:- "&TEXT(A1,"dd")&" - "&A2

k) Change the formula in (j) to as below.

="Wages for period:- "&TEXT(A1,"dd")&" - "&TEXT(A2,"dd mmmm, yyy")

l) Press Enter. You obtain the following in range A1:A4.

	A
1	1-Apr-16
2	15-Apr-16
3	
4	Wages for period:- 01 - 15 April, 2016

m) Thus, you have learned to create dynamic text.

n) For simulation, key-in "16-Apr-16" in cell A1, and "30-Apr-16" in cell A2.

o) You obtain the following in range A1:A4.

	A
1	16-Apr-16
2	30-Apr-16
3	
4	Wages for period:- 16 - 30 April, 2016

6.4 Dynamic text for report title 2

In section 6.3, we created dynamic text based on the start date and end date. These two parameters are keyed in by us. Sometimes we do not key in the start date or end date, but we key in the month and the half period (first half or second half).

In this section, the technique is quite similar to section 6.3. We still need the start date and end date. Thus, we need to create a formula to pull the start date and end date with the parameters, month, and half period.

The technique consists of four steps namely;

Step 1:- Assign the month and half period.

Step 2:- Create half period table.

Step 3:- Pull the start date and end date.

Step 4:- Convert to dynamic text.

Step 1:- Assign the month and half period.

a) Assign cell A1 for month. For a start key in "Apr".
b) Assign cell A2 for half period. For a start key in 1.
c) Create a formula in cell A3 as below.
   =A1&A2
d) Thus, cell A3 is the unique parameter.

Step 2:- Create half period table.

a) Create table as below in range J1:N25.

	J	K	L	M	N
1	Ref	Month	Half	Start	End
2		Jan	1	1-Jan	15-Jan
3		Jan	2	16-Jan	31-Jan
4		Feb	1	1-Feb	15-Feb
5		Feb	2	16-Feb	29-Feb
6		Mar	1	1-Mar	15-Mar
7		Mar	2	16-Mar	31-Mar
8		Apr	1	1-Apr	15-Apr
9		Apr	2	16-Apr	30-Apr
10		May	1	1-May	15-May
11		May	2	16-May	31-May
12		Jun	1	1-Jun	15-Jun
13		Jun	2	16-Jun	30-Jun
14		Jul	1	1-Jul	15-Jul
15		Jul	2	16-Jul	31-Jul
16		Aug	1	1-Aug	15-Aug
17		Aug	2	16-Aug	31-Aug
18		Sep	1	1-Sep	15-Sep
19		Sep	2	16-Sep	30-Sep
20		Oct	1	1-Oct	15-Oct
21		Oct	2	16-Oct	31-Oct
22		Nov	1	1-Nov	15-Nov
23		Nov	2	16-Nov	30-Nov
24		Dec	1	1-Dec	15-Dec
25		Dec	2	16-Dec	31-Dec

b) Click cell J2. Create a formula in cell J2 as below.
=K2&L2

c) Copy cell J2 to range J3:J25.

d) You obtain the following in range J1:M25.

	J	K	L	M	N
1	Ref	Month	Half	Start	End
2	Jan1	Jan	1	1-Jan	15-Jan
3	Jan2	Jan	2	16-Jan	31-Jan
4	Feb1	Feb	1	1-Feb	15-Feb
5	Feb2	Feb	2	16-Feb	29-Feb
6	Mar1	Mar	1	1-Mar	15-Mar
7	Mar2	Mar	2	16-Mar	31-Mar
8	Apr1	Apr	1	1-Apr	15-Apr
9	Apr2	Apr	2	16-Apr	30-Apr
10	May1	May	1	1-May	15-May
11	May2	May	2	16-May	31-May
12	Jun1	Jun	1	1-Jun	15-Jun
13	Jun2	Jun	2	16-Jun	30-Jun
14	Jul1	Jul	1	1-Jul	15-Jul
15	Jul2	Jul	2	16-Jul	31-Jul
16	Aug1	Aug	1	1-Aug	15-Aug
17	Aug2	Aug	2	16-Aug	31-Aug
18	Sep1	Sep	1	1-Sep	15-Sep
19	Sep2	Sep	2	16-Sep	30-Sep
20	Oct1	Oct	1	1-Oct	15-Oct
21	Oct2	Oct	2	16-Oct	31-Oct
22	Nov1	Nov	1	1-Nov	15-Nov
23	Nov2	Nov	2	16-Nov	30-Nov
24	Dec1	Dec	1	1-Dec	15-Dec
25	Dec2	Dec	2	16-Dec	31-Dec

e) Thus, range J2:J25 is the condition range.

Step 3:- Pull the start date and end date.

 a) Create a formula in cell C1 as below.
 =VLOOKUP(A3,J2:N25,4,0)
 b) Create a formula in cell C3 as below.
 =VLOOKUP(A3,J2:N25,5,0)

c) Perform date formatting, you obtain the following in range A1:C3.

	A	B	C
1	Apr		1-Apr-16
2	1		
3	Apr1		15-Apr-16

Step 4:- Convert to dynamic text.

a) Click cell A5.
b) Create a formula in cell A5as below, following the step (2) of section 8.2.
="Wages for period:- "&TEXT(C1,"dd")&" - "&TEXT(C3,"dd mmmm, yyy")
c) You obtain the following in range A1:C5.

	A	B	C
1	Apr		1-Apr-16
2	1		
3	Apr1		15-Apr-16
4			
5	Wages for period:- 01 - 15 April, 2016		

CHAPTER 7

Dynamic Total

7.0 Overview

Now you have learned how to perform a query. Remember that we fill in 1 to 10 in the range for extract data. Actually, this is the size of the extracted data. Of course, we do not use the whole size, and thus we have a blank below the data. With a blank, if we wanted to put the total just below the data, then for 10 rows, we have to put the total value at row 11. If we have 4 data, then we will have 6 blank rows before the total.

Thus, in this chapter we will learn how to put the total value just below the data. This means that even with the size of 10 rows, if we have 4 data, Excel will automatically put the total in row 5.

Using a similar idea, we can extend it to put the summary just below the extracted data.

7.1 Extract daily production output with total.

The technique consists of nine steps namely;

Step 1:- Key in the database in the spreadsheet.
Step 2:- Assign a cell for the condition.
Step 3:- Determine the number of data.
Step 4:- Determine the position of the first data.
Step 5:- Generate the rest of the data.
Step 6:- Extract data to the required range.

Step 7:- Put the total just below the extract data.
Step 8:- Extract the data together with the total.
Step 9:- Display the extract data to different sheet.

Step 1:- Key in the database in the spreadsheet.

a) Let's use the database below in range A1:D21 of Sheet1.

	A	B	C	D
1	Date	Item	Output	Reject
2	1-Mar	item1	4433	20
3	1-Mar	item2	970	1
4	1-Mar	item3	3349	31
5	1-Mar	item4	4016	20
6	1-Mar	item5	3834	2
7	1-Mar	item6	4107	4
8	2-Mar	item1	4429	42
9	3-Mar	item2	979	7
10	3-Mar	item3	3353	26
11	3-Mar	item4	4019	10
12	3-Mar	item5	3835	12
13	3-Mar	item6	4103	37
14	4-Mar	item1	4422	41
15	4-Mar	item2	977	8
16	4-Mar	item3	3338	12
17	4-Mar	item4	4011	8
18	4-Mar	item5	3827	9
19	5-Mar	item1	4428	30
20	5-Mar	item2	988	1
21	5-Mar	item3	3352	32

b) Because we are looking at the daily output, the condition must be on the date. Thus, make sure that the date data is in grouping format.

Step 2:- Assign a cell for the condition.

Assign cell F1 for keying in the condition. For a start, please key in "1-Mar" in cell F1.

Step 3:- Determine the number of data.

a) Click cell G1.
b) Create a formula in cell G1 as below.
   = COUNTIF(A1:A21,F1)
c) Press Enter. The value of cell G1 is 6.
d) This the count of data related to "1-Mar".

Step 4:- Determine the row of the first data.

a) Click cell G2.
b) Create a formula in cell G2 as below.
   =MATCH(F1,A1:A21,0)
c) Press Enter. The value of G2 is 2. This is the position of the first data in the range related to "A0001". Thus, the function =MATCH acts as a pointer.

Step 5:- Generate the rest of the data.

a) Fill in 1 to 10 in range F2:F11.
b) Click cell G3.
c) Create a formula in cell G3 as below.
   =IF(F3<=$G$1,G2+1,"")
d) Take note of the absolute cell G1.
e) Copy cell G3 to range G4:G11.
f) You obtain the following in range F1:G11.

	F	G
1	1-Mar	6
2	1	2
3	2	3
4	3	4
5	4	5
6	5	6
7	6	7
8	7	
9	8	
10	9	
11	10	

Step 6:- Extract the data accordingly.

a) Select A1:D1. Click Copy.
b) Click cell H1. Click Paste. You just copied the column heading to another range H1:K1.
c) Click cell H2.
d) Create a formula in cell H2 as below.
=HLOOKUP(H1,A1:D21,G2,0)
e) Convert the formula to absolute as below.
=HLOOKUP(H$1,$A$1:$D$21,$G2,0)
f) Notice that for cell H1, we fix only the row, and for cell G2, we fix only the column.
g) Change the formula to the following for blanking.
=IF($G2="","",HLOOKUP(H$1,$A$1:$D$21,$G2,0))
h) Copy cell H2 to range H2:K11.
i) You obtain the following in range F1:K12.

	F	G	H	I	J	K
1	1-Mar	6	Date	Item	Output	Reject
2	1	2	1-Mar	item1	4433	20
3	2	3	1-Mar	item2	970	1
4	3	4	1-Mar	item3	3349	31
5	4	5	1-Mar	item4	4016	20
6	5	6	1-Mar	item5	3834	2
7	6	7	1-Mar	item6	4107	4
8	7					
9	8					
10	9					
11	10					
12						

j) Until now, you have performed a query with grouping data. Notice that row 12 is blank.

Step 7:- Put the total just below the extract data.

a) Key in "Total" in cell I12.
b) Click cell J12.
c) Create a formula in cell J12 as below.
=SUM(J2:J11)
d) Press Enter. You obtain a value of 20709 in cell J12.
e) Copy cell J12 to cell K12.
f) You obtain a value of 78 in cell K12.
g) Now you put in the total below the extract data.

	F	G	H	I	J	K
1	1-Mar	6	Date	Item	Output	Reject
2	1	2	1-Mar	item1	4433	20
3	2	3	1-Mar	item2	970	1
4	3	4	1-Mar	item3	3349	31
5	4	5	1-Mar	item4	4016	20
6	5	6	1-Mar	item5	3834	2
7	6	7	1-Mar	item6	4107	4
8	7					
9	8					
10	9					
11	10					
12				Total	20709	78

Step 8:- Extract the data together with the total.

a) Fill in "." in cell G12.
b) Click cell N2.
c) Create a formula in cell N2 as below.
=IF(G2="","",ROW(G2))
d) Copy cell N2 to range N3:N12.
e) Click cell M2.
f) Create a formula in cell M2 as below.
=RANK(N2,$N$2:$N$12,1)
g) Copy cell M2 to range M3:M12.
h) You obtain the following in range M1:N12.

	M	N
1		
2	1	2
3	2	3
4	3	4
5	4	5
6	5	6
7	6	7
8	#VALUE!	
9	#VALUE!	
10	#VALUE!	
11	#VALUE!	
12	7	12

i) Fill in 1 to 11 in range O2:O12.

j) Click cell P2.

k) Create a formula in cell P2 as below.
    =VLOOKUP(O2,M2:N12,2,0)

l) Convert the formula to absolute as below.
    =VLOOKUP(O2,$M$2:$N$12,2,0)

m) Change the formula below for blanking.
    =IFERROR(VLOOKUP(O2,$M$2:$N$12,2,0),"")

n) Copy cell P2 to range P3:P12.

o) You obtain the following in range M1:P12.

	M	N	O	P
1				
2	1	2	1	2
3	2	3	2	3
4	3	4	3	4
5	4	5	4	5
6	5	6	5	6
7	6	7	6	7
8	#VALUE!		7	12
9	#VALUE!		8	
10	#VALUE!		9	
11	#VALUE!		10	
12	7	12	11	

p) Click cell Q2.
q) Create a formula in cell Q2 as below.
   =HLOOKUP(Q1,H1:K12,P2,0)
r) Notice that now we extract from the extracted range.
s) Convert the formula to absolute as below.
   =HLOOKUP(Q$1,$H$1:$K$12,$P2,0)
t) Change the formula to below for blanking.
   =IF($P2="","",HLOOKUP(Q$1,$H$1:$K$12,$P2,0))
u) Copy cell Q2 to range Q2:T12.
v) You will obtain the following in range O2:T12.

	O	P	Q	R	S	T
1			Date	Item	Output	Reject
2	1	2	1-Mar	item1	4433	20
3	2	3	1-Mar	item2	970	1
4	3	4	1-Mar	item3	3349	31
5	4	5	1-Mar	item4	4016	20
6	5	6	1-Mar	item5	3834	2
7	6	7	1-Mar	item6	4107	4
8	7	12	0-Jan	Total	20709	78
9	8					
10	9					
11	10					
12	11					

w) Notice that value of cell Q2 is 0-Jan. It should be blank. This is because cell H12 is empty.

x) To eliminate the 0-Jan value, click cell H12. Then press spacebar followed by Enter. Notice that the value 0-Jan becomes blank.

y) You obtain the following in range O2:T12.

	O	P	Q	R	S	T
1			Date	Item	Output	Reject
2	1	2	1-Mar	item1	4433	20
3	2	3	1-Mar	item2	970	1
4	3	4	1-Mar	item3	3349	31
5	4	5	1-Mar	item4	4016	20
6	5	6	1-Mar	item5	3834	2
7	6	7	1-Mar	item6	4107	4
8	7	12		Total	20709	78
9	8					
10	9					
11	10					
12	11					

z) For simulation, change the value of F1 to "2-Mar".

aa) You obtain the following in range O2:T12.

	O	P	Q	R	S	T
1			Date	Item	Output	Reject
2	1	2	2-Mar	item1	4429	42
3	2	12		Total	4429	42
4	3					
5	4					
6	5					
7	6					
8	7					
9	8					
10	9					
11	10					
12	11					

Step 9:- Display the extract data to different sheet.

a) Let's say you perform the dummy computation in Sheet1.
b) In Sheet2, click cell A1.
c) Create a formula in cell A1 as below.
   =Sheet1!Q1
d) Copy cell A1 to range A1:D12.
e) Goto Sheet1.
f) Click cell F2.
g) Click Cut.
h) Goto Sheet2.
i) Click cell F1.
j) Press Enter.
k) Change the format accordingly.
l) You obtain the following in range A1:F12.

⁂	A	B	C	D	E	F
1	Date	Item	Output	Reject		2-Mar
2	2-Mar	item1	4429	42		
3		Total	4429	42		
4						
5						
6						
7						
8						
9						
10						
11						
12						

m) For simulation change cell F1 to "4-Mar".

n) You obtain the following in range A1:F12.

⁂	A	B	C	D	E	F
1	Date	Item	Output	Reject		4-Mar
2	4-Mar	item1	4422	41		
3	4-Mar	item2	977	8		
4	4-Mar	item3	3338	12		
5	4-Mar	item4	4011	8		
6	4-Mar	item5	3827	9		
7		Total	16575	78		
8						
9						
10						
11						
12						

CHAPTER **8**

Dynamic Nonduplicate List

8.0 Overview

In monthly output data, we can have the same item repeated for a few days. In other words, there can be 100 rows for the output, but we have only 5 different items. Thus upon query, if we want to find the monthly summary of the 5 items, we need to manually type the 5 items and then perform the summary. This will be tedious.

In this chapter, you will learn to extract the data and remove the duplicate from the list automatically. This is a dynamic nonduplicate list.

8.1 Remove duplicate for query data

The technique consists of seven steps namely;

Step 1:- Key in the database in the spreadsheet.

Step 2:- Assign cells for the condition.

Step 3:- Determine the rows of the required data.

Step 4:- Index the position and arrange it in order.

Step 5:- Extract required field data to the required range.

Step 6:- Remove duplicate item rows.

Step 7:- Extract the nonduplicate list.

Step 1:- Key in the database in the spreadsheet.
Let's use the database below in range A1:C21 of Sheet1.

	A	B	C
1	Date	Item	Qty
2	1-Mar	item2	1326
3	1-Mar	item2	1874
4	2-Mar	item1	2000
5	2-Mar	item2	1553
6	3-Mar	item2	1362
7	3-Mar	item1	1940
8	4-Mar	item1	1349
9	6-Mar	item1	1077
10	6-Mar	item3	1511
11	7-Mar	item2	1318
12	7-Mar	item4	1059
13	7-Mar	item4	1030
14	7-Mar	item1	1307
15	7-Mar	item3	1908
16	7-Mar	item1	1415
17	8-Mar	item4	1795
18	8-Mar	item2	1251
19	9-Mar	item3	1781
20	9-Mar	item1	1847
21	10-Mar	item4	1899

Step 2:- Assign cells for the condition.

a) Assign cell F1 for start condition. For a start key in "1-Mar".
b) Assign cell F2 for end condition. For a start key in "4-Mar".
c) You obtain the following in range A1:F21.

	A	B	C	D	E	F
1	Date	Item	Qty		from	1-Mar
2	1-Mar	item2	1326		to	4-Mar
3	1-Mar	item2	1874			
4	2-Mar	item1	2000			
5	2-Mar	item2	1553			
6	3-Mar	item2	1362			
7	3-Mar	item1	1940			
8	4-Mar	item1	1349			
9	6-Mar	item1	1077			
10	6-Mar	item3	1511			
11	7-Mar	item2	1318			
12	7-Mar	item4	1059			
13	7-Mar	item4	1030			
14	7-Mar	item1	1307			
15	7-Mar	item3	1908			
16	7-Mar	item1	1415			
17	8-Mar	item4	1795			
18	8-Mar	item2	1251			
19	9-Mar	item3	1781			
20	9-Mar	item1	1847			
21	10-Mar	item4	1899			

Step 3:- Determine the rows of the required data.

a) Click cell H2.
b) Create a formula in cell H2 as below.
   =IF(AND(A2>=F1,A2<=F2),ROW(A2),"")
c) Put the absolute cell accordingly, as below.
   =IF(AND(A2>=$F$1,A2<=$F$2),ROW(A2),"")
d) Copy cell H2 to range H3:H21.
e) You should obtain the following for range E1:H21.

	E	F	G	H
1	from	1-Mar		
2	to	4-Mar		2
3				3
4				4
5				5
6				6
7				7
8				8
9				
10				
11				
12				
13				
14				
15				
16				
17				
18				
19				
20				
21				

f) For simulation, change cell F1 to "4-Mar" and cell F2 to "9-Mar".

g) You should obtain the following for range E1:H21.

▲	E	F	G	H
1	from	4-Mar		
2	to	9-Mar		
3				
4				
5				
6				
7				
8				8
9				9
10				10
11				11
12				12
13				13
14				14
15				15
16				16
17				17
18				18
19				19
20				20
21				

Step 4:- Index the position and arrange it in order.

a) Fill 1 to 20 in range I2:I21.
b) Click cell J2.
c) Create a formula in cell J2 as below.
=SMALL(H2:H21,I2)
d) Put the absolute cell accordingly, as below.
=SMALL($H$2:$H$21,I2)
e) Change a formula to as below for blanking.
=IFERROR(SMALL($H$2:$H$21,I2),"")
f) Copy cell J2 to range J3:J21.
g) You obtain the following in range E1:J21.

	E	F	G	H	I	J
1	from	4-Mar				
2	to	9-Mar			1	8
3					2	9
4					3	10
5					4	11
6					5	12
7					6	13
8				8	7	14
9				9	8	15
10				10	9	16
11				11	10	17
12				12	11	18
13				13	12	19
14				14	13	20
15				15	14	
16				16	15	
17				17	16	
18				18	17	
19				19	18	
20				20	19	
21					20	

h) For simulation, change cell F1 to "3-Mar" and cell F2 to "8-Mar".
i) You obtain the following in range E1:J21.

	E	F	G	H	I	J
1	from	3-Mar				
2	to	8-Mar			1	6
3					2	7
4					3	8
5					4	9
6				6	5	10
7				7	6	11
8				8	7	12
9				9	8	13
10				10	9	14
11				11	10	15
12				12	11	16
13				13	12	17
14				14	13	18
15				15	14	
16				16	15	
17				17	16	
18				18	17	
19					18	
20					19	
21					20	

j) Notice that I have used a different technique to extract the required rows.

Step 5:- Extract required field data to the required range.

a) Copy cell B1 to cell K1.
b) Click cell K2.
c) Create a formula in cell K2 as below.
   =HLOOKUP(K1,A1:C21,J2,0)
d) Put in absolute accordingly as below.
   =HLOOKUP(K$1,$A$1:$C$21,$J2,0)
e) Change the formula to as below for blanking.
   =IF(J2="","",HLOOKUP(K$1,$A$1:$C$21,$J2,0))

139

f) Copy cell K2 to range K3:K21.
g) You obtain the following in range E1:K21.

	E	F	G	H	I	J	K
1	from	3-Mar					Item
2	to	8-Mar			1	6	item2
3					2	7	item1
4					3	8	item1
5					4	9	item1
6				6	5	10	item3
7				7	6	11	item2
8				8	7	12	item4
9				9	8	13	item4
10				10	9	14	item1
11				11	10	15	item3
12				12	11	16	item1
13				13	12	17	item4
14				14	13	18	item2
15				15	14		
16				16	15		
17				17	16		
18				18	17		
19					18		
20					19		
21					20		

Step 6:- Remove duplicate item rows.

a) Click cell L2.
b) Create a formula in cell L2 as below.
=COUNTIF(K2:K2,K2)
c) Put in absolute accordingly as below.
=COUNTIF($K$2:K2,K2)
d) Change the formula to as below for blanking.
=IF(K2="","",COUNTIF($K$2:K2,K2))
e) Copy cell L2 to range L3:L21.
f) You obtain the following in range I1:L21.

140

	I	J	K	L
1			Item	
2	1	6	item2	1
3	2	7	item1	1
4	3	8	item1	2
5	4	9	item1	3
6	5	10	item3	1
7	6	11	item2	2
8	7	12	item4	1
9	8	13	item4	2
10	9	14	item1	4
11	10	15	item3	2
12	11	16	item1	5
13	12	17	item4	3
14	13	18	item2	3
15	14			
16	15			
17	16			
18	17			
19	18			
20	19			
21	20			

g) Create a formula in cell M2.
=IF(L2=1,ROW(L2),"")

h) Copy cell M2 to range M3:M21.

i) Create a formula in cell N2 as below.
=SMALL(M2:M21,I2)

j) Put in absolute accordingly as below.
=SMALL($M$2:$M$21,I2)

k) Change formula to as below for blanking.
=IFERROR(SMALL($M$2:$M$21,I2),"")

l) Copy cell M2 to range M3:M21.

m) You obtain the following in range J1:M21.

	J	K	L	M	N
1		Item			
2	6	item2	1	2	2
3	7	item1	1	3	3
4	8	item1	2		6
5	9	item1	3		8
6	10	item3	1	6	
7	11	item2	2		
8	12	item4	1	8	
9	13	item4	2		
10	14	item1	4		
11	15	item3	2		
12	16	item1	5		
13	17	item4	3		
14	18	item2	3		
15	19	item3	3		
16	20	item1	6		
17					
18					
19					
20					
21					

n) Note that we have four nonduplicate items (column N).
o) For simulation, change cell F1 to "1-Mar" and cell F2 to "6-Mar".
p) You obtain the following in range J1:M21.

	I	J	K	L	M	N
1			Item			
2	1	2	item2	1	2	2
3	2	3	item2	2		4
4	3	4	item1	1	4	10
5	4	5	item2	3		
6	5	6	item2	4		
7	6	7	item1	2		
8	7	8	item1	3		
9	8	9	item1	4		
10	9	10	item3	1	10	
11	10					
12	11					
13	12					
14	13					
15	14					
16	15					
17	16					
18	17					
19	18					
20	19					
21	20					

q) Note that we have three nonduplicate items (column N).

Step 7:- Extract the nonduplicate list.

a) Copy cell K1 to cell O1.
b) Click cell O2.
c) Create a formula in cell O2 as below
   =HLOOKUP(O1,K1:K21,N2,0)
d) Put in absolute accordingly as below.
   =HLOOKUP(O$1,$K$1:$K$21,$N2,0)
e) Change the formula as below for blanking.
   =IF(N2="","",HLOOKUP(O$1,$K$1:$K$21,$N2,0))
f) Copy cell O2 to range O3:O21.

g) You obtain the following in range I1:O21.

	I	J	K	L	M	N	O
1			Item				Item
2	1	2	item2	1	2	2	item2
3	2	3	item2	2		4	item1
4	3	4	item1	1	4	10	item3
5	4	5	item2	3			
6	5	6	item2	4			
7	6	7	item1	2			
8	7	8	item1	3			
9	8	9	item1	4			
10	9	10	item3	1	10		
11	10						
12	11						
13	12						
14	13						
15	14						
16	15						
17	16						
18	17						
19	18						
20	19						
21	20						

h) For simulation, change cell F2 to "10-Mar".
i) You obtain the following in range I1:O21.

	I	J	K	L	M	N	O
1			Item				Item
2	1	2	item2	1	2	2	item2
3	2	3	item2	2		4	item1
4	3	4	item1	1	4	10	item3
5	4	5	item2	3		12	item4
6	5	6	item2	4			
7	6	7	item1	2			
8	7	8	item1	3			
9	8	9	item1	4			
10	9	10	item3	1	10		
11	10	11	item2	5			
12	11	12	item4	1	12		
13	12	13	item4	2			
14	13	14	item1	5			
15	14	15	item3	2			
16	15	16	item1	6			
17	16	17	item4	3			
18	17	18	item2	6			
19	18	19	item3	3			
20	19	20	item1	7			
21	20	21	item4	4			

j) Notice that although you have twenty data, but only four are nonduplicate items.

k) Starting from the nonduplicate list (column N), you can create a normal Excel formula using the list.

www.ingramcontent.com/pod-product-compliance
Lightning Source LLC
LaVergne TN
LVHW091940060326
832903LV00043B/7